What others are saying about this book:

"Silverman provides not only useful but essential guidance to college faculty and other professionals interested in a respectable and increasingly popular alternative to commercial publishing houses. I recommend this book highly to any author who is interested in publishing his or her own material."

—John F. Wakefield, Professor of Education,
University of North Alabama

"I wish this book had been available before I started self-publishing. It describes almost all the ins and outs of self-publishing that I have encountered, plus many more. With self-publishing becoming more popular and acceptable, it seems that any writer would benefit from the knowledge that is locked within the pages of Dr. Silverman's book."

—Jerome A. Halvorson, Professor of Communicative
Disorders, University of Wisconsin-River Falls

"Using both his own and others' experience, Dr. Silverman presents a practical, highly readable overview of the entire self-publishing process. The book is quite thorough and gives equal weight to the arguments for and against academic self-publishing. There are practical suggestions, cautions, and examples. Any academic author contemplating self-publishing should purchase this book and study it carefully."

—Robert D. Moulton, Graduate Dean,
New Mexico State University

"I cannot think of anyone more qualified to write this book than Frank Silverman. He is a well respected, much published academic author.... His knowledge and experience in academic writing have been of immeasurable assistance to many a writer in the Text and Academic Authors Association, and he is an inspiration to all of us who know him. Dig into Frank's *Self-Publishing Textbooks and Instructional Materials*, and you will be rewarded with sound advice—solid gold!"

—Ronald E. Pynn, Executive Director,

Text and Academic Authors

"In this book Frank Silverman shares advice that works every time. It's an immensely valuable how-to book.... He was among the early experts on self-publishing technology, which allows writers to leapfrog vexatious publishers to reach readers. Not only does Frank know the ins and outs of self-publishing, he has done it, self-publishing book after book. Though a prolific self-publisher, Frank simultaneously issued books through traditional publishing channels and kept in touch with that side of authoring also."

—John Vivian, President, Society of Academic Authors

"This reference book by Frank Silverman is a fine testament to the feasibility and value of self-publishing, a subject dear to my heart. As the self-published author of *The Self-Publishing Manual: How to Write, Print and Sell Your Own Book*, now in its 14th revised edition since 1979, I am always glad to see a self-published book succeed. Frank's new title is sure to be among those books, especially as he says my work inspired him to write it!"

—Dan Poynter, Author and Publisher,

The Self-Publishing Manual

Self-Publishing Textbooks and Instructional Materials

A Practical Guide to Successful—and Respectable—Self-Publishing

Franklin H. Silverman, Ph.D.

Foreword by Dan Poynter

ATLANTIC PATH
PUBLISHING

Self-Publishing Textbooks and Instructional Materials
A Practical Guide to Successful—and Respectable—Self-Publishing
By Franklin H. Silverman
Copyright © 2004 by Atlantic Path Publishing

Atlantic Path Publishing, P.O. Box 1556, Gloucester, MA 01931-1556
www.atlanticpathpublishing.com
Phone: 978-283-1531   Fax: 866-640-1412
Email: contactus@atlanticpathpublishing.com

Edited by Mary Ellen Lepionka
Cover and Book Design by Stevens Brosnihan

Library of Congress Control Number: 2003115614
ISBN: 0-9728164-3-7
Printed in USA

Publisher's Cataloging-in-Publication Data
(Prepared by The Donohue Group, Inc.)

Silverman, Franklin H.
   Self-publishing textbooks and instructional materials : a practical guide to successful--and respectable--self-publishing / Franklin H. Silverman ; foreword by Dan Poynter.
      p. cm.
   Includes bibliographical references and index.
   ISBN: 0-9728164-3-7
1. Self-publishing--Handbooks, manuals, etc. 2. Textbooks--Publishing. 3. New business enterprises--Management. I. Poynter, Dan. II. Title.

Z285.5 .S55 2004
070.5'93—-dc21 2003115614

CONTENTS

LIST OF ILLUSTRATIONS AND TABLES

Foreword by Dan Poynter

This reference book by Frank Silverman is a fine testament to the feasibility and value of self-publishing, a subject dear to my heart. As the self-published author of *The Self-Publishing Manual: How to Write, Print and Sell Your Own Book*, now in its 14th revised edition since 1979, I am always glad to see a self-published book succeed. Frank's new title is sure to be among those books, especially as he says my work inspired him to write it!

Frank has published many academic books in his field—speech pathology--with commercial publishers, but also self-published the book on which his new title is based (*Self-Publishing Books and Materials for Students, Academics, and Professionals*, CODI Publications, 2000). In addition, Frank has been conducting campus workshops on self-publishing since the mid-1980s under the auspices of the Text and Academic Authors Association and various universities. His new book is an outgrowth of that experience—in addition to any inspiration I may have provided.

The new book, *Self-Publishing Textbooks and Instructional Materials,* is written from the perspective of the academic author. It carries the essential self-publishing message to an important new audience: academics, professionals, scholars, and instructors who want to self-publish their work for one another or for their students. Because of recent publishing industry trends and advances in technology, academic self-publishing today probably is more possible—and more desirable—and even potentially more profitable--than at any other time in history.

While Frank's book focuses on instructional materials for higher education, it also covers the print and electronic self-publishing of scholarly works and nonfiction trade books. All this is done in the most practical of terms but also without neglecting the philosophical side of things. An entire chapter is devoted to the question of academic respectability in self-publishing, for example, and readers also reflect on their attitudes and values about disseminating their scholarship, the scholarship of education, and publishing as a business enterprise.

After dealing with intellectual matters, Frank guides readers through the physical acts of self-publishing--chronologically, step-by-step--explaining all the decision points. His book offers detailed, succinct, practical advice at every turn. The book covers everything from setting up one's own publishing company to selling subsidiary and reprint rights. In between, Frank discusses "everything else," for example, how to choose projects for self-publishing, generate working capital, draft text, do an index, secure permissions, obtain registrations, prepare an ebook, evaluate a book design, perform typesetting on the computer, choose a printer, market and promote successfully, etc., etc., etc.

I was glad to see that *Self-Publishing Textbooks and Instructional Materials* treats all prospective self-publishers equally, recognizing the many different reasons for publishing that an academic or professional might have. There is information on how to publish a four-color case-bound nationally distributed textbook for an undergraduate course as well as on how to publish a 64-page spiral-bound camera-ready print-on-demand supplement or training manual for a small or restricted audience.

I was also glad to see that this book does not attempt to explain every little nuance of self-publishing—this can be a trap, I know! Rather, in the best reference tradition, Frank anticipates questions and coaches readers on where to go for more answers. And, in keeping with the advances of the Information Age, some of those answers—including links to resources cited in the book--are collected on the publisher's web site, www.atlanticpathpublishing.com, which provides open access to the information.

My self-publishing adventures have produced more than 100 books in the areas I know and love best—publishing and skydiving—and a career in seminars and speaking. In a way, Frank's new book reminds me of the connection I see between skydiving and self-publishing: You have to pack your parachute properly and well, get professional back-up, choose the right spot, be willing to take the leap, enjoy the effort and the thrill--and have a way to get home. Maybe *Self-Publishing Textbooks and Academic Materials* should have a subtitle: *Skydiving for Author-Publishers?*

In any event, congratulations to Frank Silverman and Atlantic Path Publishing on a fine contribution to the self-publishing literature, and best of luck from

Dan Poynter, The Self-Publishing Manual,
http://ParaPublishing.com

Foreword by Ronald Pynn

Reading a book is like digging a well. You never can be sure what you are going to find. Most often you find water. After all, that is what you were looking for in the first place. Sometimes, all you get is another spade full of dirt, as the effort produces nothing of substance. But then there are occasions when you strike gold, when you find an unexpected treasure for all your digging. Sheer joy comes from having made the effort. Readers of Franklin Silverman's *Self-Publishing Textbooks and Instructional Materials* are going to find gold.

First, Frank Silverman is a veteran "well digger." He is the author of two dozen texts and academic books along with some 150 professional articles. He has received numerous recognitions and awards, including Saudi Arabia's prize for Scientific Research on Rehabilitation and the Text and Academic Authors Association (TAA) Lifetime Achievement Award. More to the point, Frank Silverman is a self-published author, establishing and operating his own publishing company—CODI Publications. In addition, on behalf of TAA he conducts workshops on authoring an academic book and on self-publishing.

Silverman notes there are several books on self-publishing on the market, but all are for trade books. His *Self-Publishing Textbooks and Instructional Materials* looks at self-publishing for the more specialized academic market. In doing so he has filled a void and given balance to the self-publishing phenomenon that is growing in both popularity and stature.

Readers will discover how Frank Silverman clears away much of the outdated and outmoded thinking about self-publishing, especially regarding academic respectability. This alone makes the book golden. But readers also will find in this work that Frank unearths practical guidelines for self-publishing as well. If you want to know how to create sophisticated designs, printings, graphics, covers, and bindings to rival those of any major publishing house, *Self-Publishing Textbooks and Instructional Materials* is a must book! There are practical "how to" guides for such topics as marketing, file formatting, graphics, page design, printing on demand, copy editing, and, of course, financial considerations.

While the book focuses on "how to" establish, write, and print your own instructional materials, Silverman makes an important distinction between process and product. The process of self-publishing is becoming more academically respectable, but this does not guarantee that the product will be respectable. Authors and academicians need to take the same care with self-publishing that they do with journal writing and conference papers. In fact, Frank makes an important parallel between the two processes. Indeed, Frank points out ways to assure academic integrity as a self-publisher, while also noting the possible academic pitfalls.

I cannot think of anyone more qualified to write this book than Frank Silverman. He is a well respected, much published academic author. Frank and I go way back in our association with TAA, from the organization's earliest years. His knowledge and experience in academic writing has been of immeasurable assistance to many a writer in TAA, and he is an inspiration to all of us who know him. Dig into Frank's *Self-Publishing Textbooks and Instructional Materials*, and you will be rewarded with sound advice—solid gold!

Ronald E. Pynn, Executive Director

Text and Academic Authors Association

Foreword by John Vivian

Never have I met anyone so passionate about writing as Frank Silverman. Nor as curious. He writes every day, a pre-dawn ritual. Beyond being a writer, Frank has wanted to know what makes writers tick. Many years ago he told me he had surveyed writers about their habits and found far fewer addicted to a pre-dawn habit than he expected. In fact, the diversity in approaches surprised him. Frank enjoyed telling about one writer who donned a tuxedo to approach the keyboard—and another who could write only in the nude.

Idiosyncrasies aside, Frank knows there are more dead-end and disastrous ways than successful ones for writing textbooks and instructional materials and then self-publishing them. In this book Frank Silverman shares advice that works every time. It is an immensely valuable how-to book.

Frank Silverman has always been one to speak out. As a speech pathology scholar, he exposed abuses that had occurred in human research with speech-impaired people, and his revelations made national headlines. And he believes in what he does. Although Jewish, he had no reservations about traveling to the Middle East to help Arab children overcome speech difficulties. Because he shared his knowledge to help the children, he was honored by the government of Saudi Arabia and by Palestinian leader Yasser Arafat.

As a writer also, Frank Silverman has been in the habit of sharing. He has traversed the country conducting workshops for aspiring academic writers. Sometimes he has accepted honorariums, sometimes not. Money is not the issue. Rather, he has something to share and revels in the opportunity. His curriculum vita is heavy with articles he has produced on writing for members of author organizations. On the Society of Academic Authors web site, we have what is called the Silverman Collection (**sa2.info/HOW-TO/howtoindex.html**).

Frank's *Self-Publishing Textbooks and Instructional Materials* is an honest appraisal. He is clear about the downsides, including financial risks, market forces, trade barriers, and publisher insensitivity to authors; but Frank always sees possibilities. He was among the early experts on self-publishing technology, which allows writers to leapfrog vexatious publishers to reach readers. Not only does Frank know the ins and outs of self-publishing, he has done it, self-publishing book after book. Though a prolific self-publisher, Frank simultaneously issued books through traditional publishing channels and kept in touch with that side of authoring also.

A mark of Frank's success in tutoring literally dozens of authors is the clarity with which he organizes his material. This book, like his articles and workshops, is no exception. His points are crystallized in nuggets, concise and clearly labeled, which makes the book useful as a reference in the future as well as a valuable and good read the first time through.

John Vivian, Founder and President
Society of Academic Authors

AUTHOR'S PREFACE

Publishers of textbooks and instructional materials unfortunately have become very "bottom line" oriented. To get a publishing contract for such a book or material now, you usually have to be able to document not only that it is likely to be academically respectable and make a worthwhile contribution, but also that it is likely to yield an adequate financial return for the publisher. This is true even for many university presses, because their long-term survival is dependent on their not being a financial drain on their institution.

Publishers can be found for most educational books and materials that are academically respectable and likely to make a worthwhile contribution. There are some, however, for which a publisher is unlikely to be found. The reason may be that the number of copies likely to be sold is too small to yield an adequate financial return for a publisher. Or it may be that the market is probably sufficiently large to yield an adequate financial return for a publisher, but the author is unable to document this before the book is published. Or the author could attract a publisher but chooses not to do so. For such books and materials, there is an academically respectable option that may be affordable and profitable as well—i.e., self-publishing.

Self-publishing has been a respectable option for initially getting books into print since the founding of this country. Benjamin Franklin initially self-published *Poor Richard's Almanac,* and Mark Twain initially self-published *Huckleberry Finn.* Other well-known books that were initially self-published include *Robert's Rules of Order* and *Bartlett's Quotations.* Two of the most successful college textbooks in my field were initially self-published. And an academic book that I initially self-published—*Authoring Books and Materials for Students, Academics, and Professionals*—was later published in 1998 by Praeger.

A college teacher who wants to self-publish a book or material shouldn't have to reinvent the wheel. While there are several books in print that focus on self-publishing trade books, none have as a primary focus self-publishing textbooks and instructional materials. This book is intended to fill this void. Specifically, it is intended to provide the practical how-to information needed to successfully self-publish textbooks and instructional materials for students.

This book is intended to serve as a model as well as a how-to guide. The design, printing, and binding of a self-published book can be as sophisticated as any published by an educational book publisher, although producing textbooks with a high level of sophistication tends to be expensive and traditionally requires a fairly large first printing to keep per-copy production costs reasonable. For books that consist mainly of text and are purchased for their content, an affordable alternative approach to designing, printing, and binding them is having copies "printed on demand" (POD).

It is not possible to give credit to the many sources from which the ideas in this book have been drawn. This book is the result of years of involvement with writing and publishing and hundreds of hours of conversations with persons engaged in these activities, particularly members of the Text and Academic Authors Association. I would like to thank my editor and publisher, Mary Ellen Lepionka, who helped to make this book as accurate and up to date as possible, and artist Stevens Brosnihan, who designed a splendid cover and interior as well as the graphics.

I especially would like to thank my mentor and colleagues who wrote forewords for this edition of *Self-Publishing Textbooks and Instructional Materials*. Dan Poynter of Para Publishing is known throughout the industry for *The Self-Publishing Manual* and his many related books and articles championing small presses and self-publishers. From the beginning his works have guided me in my self-publishing ventures. Ronald Pynn, Executive Director of the Text and Academic Authors Association, and John Vivian, President of the Society of Academic Authors, have been both my colleagues and my friends. Their comments about me and my work gladden the heart.

Finally, I welcome feedback from readers about this book and its contents, as well as suggestions for the support web page at **www.atlanticpathpublishing.com**. Please forward comments and suggestions to the publisher via the web site or at Atlantic Path Publishing, P.O. Box 1556, Gloucester, MA 01931-1556. Meanwhile, I wish you the best of luck in your self-publishing project.

Franklin H. Silverman

Greendale, WI

September 15, 2003

About the Author

Franklin H. Silverman is a Professor of Speech Pathology at Marquette University (Milwaukee, Wisconsin) and a Clinical Professor of Rehabilitation Medicine at the Medical College of Wisconsin (Wauwatosa, Wisconsin). He has authored more than 150 papers in professional journals and 14 major books: *Legal-Ethical Considerations, Restrictions, and Obligations for Clinicians who Treat Communicative Disorders* (Second Edition, 1992, Charles C. Thomas), *Speech, Language, and Hearing Disorders* (Second Edition, 1995, Allyn & Bacon), *Communication for the Speechless* (Third Edition, 1995, Allyn & Bacon), *Stuttering and Other Fluency Disorders* (Second Edition, 1996, Allyn & Bacon), *Computer Applications for Augmenting the Management of Speech, Language, and Hearing Disorders* (Second Edition, 1997, Allyn & Bacon), *Research Design and Evaluation in Speech-Language Pathology and Audiology* (Fourth Edition, 1998, Allyn & Bacon), *Authoring Books and Materials for Students, Academics, and Professionals* (1998, Praeger), *Fundamentals of Electronics for Speech-Language Pathologists and Audiologists* (1999, Allyn & Bacon), *Professional Issues in Speech-Language Pathology and Audiology* (1999, Allyn & Bacon), *The Telecommunication Relay Service (TRS) Handbook* (1999, Aegis), *Publishing for Tenure and Beyond* (1999, Praeger), *Publishing for Teaching and Beyond* (2001, Bergin & Garvey), *Essentials of Speech,, Language,, and Hearing Disorders* (2003, Atomic Dog), and *Essentials of Professional Issues in Speech-Language Pathology and Audiology* (2003, Waveland).

One of his books has been a Main Selection and three have been Alternate Selections in professional book clubs. Translations of several of his books have been published. Since the early 1980s, he has occasionally self-published textbooks and instructional materials and has offered "how to" workshops on self-publishing.

Dr. Silverman is a Fellow of both the American Speech-Language-Hearing Association and the Text and Academic Authors Association and a recipient of the Marquette University Faculty Award for Teaching Excellence, Emerson College's Alumni Achievement Award, the Disabled Children's Association of Saudi Arabia's Prize for Scientific Research on Rehabilitation, the Text and Academic Authors Association's Lifetime Achievement Award, and in 2003 the Texty Textbook Excellent Award for his first edition of *Essentials of*

Speech, Language, and Hearing Disorders (Atomic Dog). His biography has appeared in *Who's Who in the Midwest, Who's Who in America, Who's Who in the World, Who's Who in Medicine and Healthcare,* and *Who's Who in World Jewry.* He has been conducting academic and professional book authoring and publishing workshops since the mid-1980s under the auspices of the Text and Academic Authors Association, where he is a Past President, and several universities.

In March of 2003 Frank Silverman was diagnosed with a cancerous brain tumor that ultimately proved inoperable. Undaunted, he worked to the last to revise and update all his books and to find publishing venues for his new projects, including this book, which is based on a self-published work that he distributed through his authoring workshops. In August 2003 in a candid interview with Douglas L. Beck, President and Editor-in-Chief of Speech Pathology Online (http://www.speechpathology.com, quoted with permission), Dr. Silverman talked about "Dying Well." When asked about "the silver lining," he said:

> The positives are that I get to really concentrate on developing closer relationships. The family became closer. I had time to heal and focus on relationships…. Everyone doesn't get to do that…. One thing that was amusing is that because I know I am going to die sooner rather than later, I wanted to pick my memorial stone. As you might guess, I got the sample book. Then I had to pick the box, the location, and so many details I never thought much about before. Finally, I decided to have them write, "He taught. He wrote. He helped"…. I'm feeling very fortunate for the time I have had and the time I have left.

Frank Silverman died at home several months later at the age of 70, his wife and children by his side. He did not live to see this book in print but authorized future editions under the publisher's coauthorship.

Self-Publishing Is Academically Respectable

Many college faculty tend to assume that if a textbook or instructional material for college students is well written and worthwhile, it should be possible to find a publisher for it. Furthermore, they tend to assume that if you have to publish it yourself, there must be something wrong with it and, consequently, the publication isn't worthy to be considered academically respectable. If you tend to make such assumptions and are willing to read this chapter with an open mind, your beliefs about the respectability of at least some self-published textbooks and materials may be challenged.

Are Good Books Self-Published?

Self-publishing is not a recent phenomenon. It has existed for hundreds of years. The following are books that were initially self-published and are now almost universally regarded as respectable: *The Elements of Style* (William Strunk, Jr., and E. B. White); *Familiar Quotations* (John Bartlett); *Robert's Rules of Order* (Henry M. Roberts); *Poor Richard's Almanack* (Benjamin Franklin); and *Huckleberry Finn* (Mark Twain). Other well-known books that were originally self-published include the *Tarzan* series (Edgar Rice Burroughs); *Ulysses* (James Joyce); *Lady Chatterly's Lover* (D.H. Lawrence); *Leaves of Grass* (Walt Whitman); *The Jungle* (Upton Sinclair); and *A Week on the Concord and Merrimack Rivers* (Henry Thoreau). These books were all later acquired and reprinted by publishers. This, incidentally, is not an unusual occurrence. Two of my self-published books (Silverman, 1998 and 2000) have been acquired by academic publishers and republished. Self-publishing books is perhaps even more respectable now than it was previously. In a segment dealing with publishing trends on CNN (May 12, 1997), it was revealed that major bookstores—such as Barnes & Noble—are now selling large numbers of self-published books.

Surveys of members of the Text and Academic Authors Association (TAA)—an organization that represents textbook and other academic authors in the United States—suggest that significant numbers of instructors and scholars have self-published books. The fact that the books were self-published may not be known to readers, because they probably were published and marketed by a company the author set up for the purpose and because their printing and binding are similar to those of some other academic books. The reason for the similarity is that most textbook and academic publishers do not do all the various production tasks for their books in house. They contract with freelancers and packagers or printers to do them, and self-publishers can use the same services.

Self-Publishing Versus Vanity Publishing

Because of the assumption that self-published books and materials are lacking in some way, self-publishing tends to be equated with vanity press publishing. While in both instances the author pays to have his or her work published, there are several significant differences. First, vanity presses make their money from authors, and self-publishers make their money from readers. Vanity (subsidy) presses make a profit by charging authors more than it costs them to produce their book. Few of the books they publish are of interest to more than a handful of people. Consequently, it is not surprising that the average author who publishes with such a firm gets a return of only about $.25 on each dollar of his or her subsidy (Ross & Ross, 1994). The person's payoff is an expression of vanity—being able to regard himself or herself as a published author and being so regarded by his or her family and friends.

A second difference between vanity press publishing and self-publishing is that books published by vanity presses are likely to be assumed to be of low quality, while those that are published by small presses established by self-publishers are not usually evaluated in this way. It would definitely not enhance your national reputation as a scholar to have a book published by a vanity press. Worse, if you are an assistant professor, having such a publication could do you harm when you go up for tenure because at least one person who evaluates your application is likely to recognize the publisher as a vanity press.

A book published by a university press that the author was required to partially subsidize is not regarded the same way in academia as one published by a vanity press. This type of subsidy is sometimes referred to as an author subvention (Parsons, 1989). Its purpose is to enable the press to afford to publish a book that is likely to have low sales because the topic is of interest to only a relatively small number of students or other persons.

Acquisitions, the Bottom Line, and Book Publishing

Finding a publisher for a textbook or instructional material that is unlikely to become a best seller is becoming more and more difficult. This situation, unfortunately, is unlikely to improve. Perhaps the main reason is the acquisition of companies publishing textbooks and instructional materials by other publishers. When a large textbook publisher acquires another, there are several likely consequences. First, when they combine their publication lists, they are likely to find duplication. That is, they have two or more textbooks for the same segment of a course market or two or more professional books on the same topic. One way that publishers solve this problem is allowing some books to die a slow death by making no real effort to market them and then declining to publish a revision.

Nastier solutions may involve having sales representatives actually discourage faculty from adopting the unrevised textbook by indicating, for example, that it is out of date. This tactic builds up the representative's credibility, making faculty believe that the company really is trying to be helpful and not merely interested in sales. The publisher furthermore may not return the copyright to the author in a timely manner, to prevent him or her from contracting with another publisher for a revised edition. The publisher may refuse to release a book to its author by declaring it out of print, even when the title is selling only a few copies a year. In these ways, publishers can avoid having to compete for adoptions with a revised edition of a book they published.

Other textbooks that are acquired through mergers and acquisitions can also meet the same fate. The new editor responsible for a book may not be particularly interested in it nor bonded with its authors. The new editor even could receive a bonus by acquiring a new title to replace it. Consequently, the new editor may not be strongly motivated to promote the book, particularly if it is not a blockbuster book. Another consequence of mergers is that the resulting company tends to publish fewer books than the individual companies did previously. Thus, textbook authors find fewer publishers in their specialties, and textbook consumers find fewer choices.

The acquisition of a book publisher by a large corporation to improve its bottom line can reduce opportunities for publishing textbooks and instructional materials that are not regarded as having the potential to become best sellers. College textbooks regarded as having this potential tend to be ones for large-enrollment undergraduate courses. Texts for upper-division undergraduate and graduate courses will, of course, continue to be published. However, finding a publisher for them is likely to become more and more difficult because of increasing concern about bottom-line profitability. This is particularly true for texts that differ significantly in organization, content, or philosophy from the competition. Such books are likely to be regarded as risky to publish, even if they more accurately reflect the existing state of knowledge or an emerging consensus in a field. Instructors who adopt different textbooks probably will have to significantly modify their course syllabi, which will tend to discourage many from doing so.

Self-Publishing: Process Versus Product

To answer this chapter's central question—Is self-publishing academically respectable?—we must distinguish between the process of self-publishing and the product—i.e., the book or material that is self-published. While self-publishing, as a process, is academically respectable, a book or material that is self-published may not be.

All college and university faculty self-publish materials, including the course syllabi and handouts they author. Few faculty consider their course syllabi and handouts to be publications, however, because these materials are not typeset and probably are not sold. Nevertheless, they are classified as publications by U.S. copyright law. Neither typesetting nor selling a document is a requirement for it to be a publication. Faculty also self-publish in their role as scholars. Many (perhaps most), for example, distribute copies of their conference and convention papers. Furthermore, some distribute preprints of articles they have submitted (or intend to submit) to journals.

While faculty consider it academically respectable to self-publish course syllabi, handouts, convention papers, and preprints, they might not regard all such self-published works as academically respectable. The appearance of publications and the value of the information they contain vary considerably. Some might be so unprofessional in appearance or the quality of the information in them of so little value that few, if any, academics would consider them respectable.

This, of course, is also true for the publications of textbook publishers. While the appearance of almost all the books and materials they publish appears sufficiently professional to be labeled as respectable, this is not necessarily the case for their content. The information in some of the books and materials they publish is of so little value that few, if any, college teachers would adopt them for use in a course.

Perhaps the best way to answer our question (Is self-publishing academically respectable?) is to say that the process is academically respectable, but the product may not be. Strong evidence for academic respectability of the process is the fact that all college faculty do it. That is, they all self-publish course syllabi and handouts and many also self-publish convention (conference) papers and distribute preprints. If the process were not academically respectable, it wouldn't be so commonplace. Procedures to also guaranteeing the academic respectability of the product also exist, fortunately, such as peer reviewing.

This chapter has viewed self-publishing textbooks and instructional materials as an option, but it also can be viewed as an educational obligation. Because of the bottom-line business mentality of most textbook publishers, information you have that could be helpful to your students or academic or professional peers may not be available to them unless you self-publish it.

Self-Publishing Has Potential Benefits and Risks

Self-publishing, like all activities, has risks and can yield both benefits and losses. If you find that the potential benefits of self-publishing a textbook or academic material appear to outweigh the risks, then self-publishing is worth considering. However, you also will need to determine the benefit/risk ratio for self-publishing each particular book or material, because this ratio is unlikely to be the same for every project. That is, self-publishing could be advantageous in some cases and not in others.

There are a number of ways that you can gain or lose by self-publishing a textbook or instructional material. Ways that are among the most relevant for college instructors are indicated in this chapter along with factors to weigh when considering options—i.e., determining the benefit/risk ratio for a particular project. This information should help you when deciding whether to self-publish a particular project.

Potential Benefits of Self-Publishing

Many academics have self-published more than one academic work. They did so again because the benefits they derived from doing so outweighed the losses. This is certainly the reason that I have continued to self-publish. Some of the benefits from self-publishing include the following.

- Providing information or tools that otherwise might not be available to others
- Retaining control over price, form, length, and

content

- Making it unnecessary to cope with contractual matters, such as the "satisfactory manuscript" clause
- Controlling the length of time that a textbook or instructional material stays in print
- Authorizing revisions to keep textbooks and instructional materials current
- Retaining the copyright
- Controlling reprint rights
- Shortening the time lag between the completion of a project and its publication
- Generating greater income than from royalties and rights sales
- Controlling marketing and promotion
- Learning new skills
- Benefiting indirectly from family participation
- Having pleasure!

This list is not intended to be exhaustive or to dictate priorities. Implications of these items are considered next.

Providing Information Not Otherwise Available

Textbook publishers, because of their bottom-line orientation, may be unwilling to publish some textbooks and instructional materials that could be helpful (perhaps even extremely helpful) to students. One reason may be that their author(s) are unable to document a market of adequate size for publishing to be profitable. By self-publishing such a textbook or instructional material, you are likely to make a contribution (perhaps even a substantial one) to your field. Another reason may be that the publisher rejected the manuscript because some of the material was highly controversial—i.e., not mainstream or politically correct. Self-publishing might enable you to contribute nationally to the discussion of issues about which you have strong feelings.

Controlling Price, Form, Length, and Content

The publisher has the final word on the form, content, and length of a book or material. Consequently, if the author is not the publisher and the author and publisher disagree on cost, form, length, and/or content, the publisher's preferences usually will prevail. Decisions that textbook publishers make regarding cost, form, length, and content usually are dictated mainly by what customers want or expect. Another factor is the amount of income that a book or material has to generate to be profitable. Furthermore, the publisher may require a book to be a particular length so that it can be sold for a particular price. Length is determined through research on what customers regard as appropriate for a course.

The content of a book also can be influenced by a publisher's bottom line. To maximize adoptions of a textbook, for example, a publisher may insist that the content and organization be traditional. A publisher may also insist that any points of view (or biases) the author has that could reduce adoptions be eliminated. However, it is possible that the author's points of view, which must be declared, are more strongly supported by research than traditional views.

Avoiding the "Satisfactory Manuscript" Clause

All book and material publishing contracts contain what is referred to as the "satisfactory manuscript" clause. This clause states that the publisher can refuse to publish a book or material that, in its judgment, is not satisfactory in form and/or content. Some manuscripts are substandard and not salable as written. However, publishers have unfortunately misused this clause to escape having to publish books and materials for reasons not legitimately related to form or content. Textbook publishers have been known to use the satisfactory manuscript clause to escape having to publish a book for any reason. Perhaps the market for that book has been satisfied by another one of the publisher's titles, for instance. Or the cost of publishing the work will make it unprofitable. Some publishers invoking the satisfactory manuscript clause even demand that the author return his or her advance with interest!

If you are planning to self-publish a textbook or instructional material, you will not have this problem. You are the one who decides whether the book or material gets published. You can publish it even if the niche it was intended to fill is considerably smaller than when you began the project. And you are the one—for better or worse—who judges the quality of your work.

Controlling How Long the Work Is In Print

A textbook publisher may declare a book or material out of print when it no longer sells a particular number of copies in a year. For a textbook, this number can be as low as 500. A self-publisher can keep a book or material in print for as long as it sells any copies, however, particularly if individual copies are printed on demand or in short print runs or if the book or material is distributed electronically (e.g., as downloadable files on the Internet).

It can be disadvantageous to you, incidentally, if your publisher keeps your textbook or instructional material in print indefinitely by using print-on-demand (POD) technology. Your publisher could then reduce competition for one of its other textbooks by preventing yours from being revised and marketed by another publisher. A self-publisher would never run into this situation, because he or she would own the copyright and could, therefore, revise and market the book or material in any lawful way that he or she desired.

Authorizing Revisions

A textbook publisher is unlikely to permit a book or material to be revised unless it is selling a certain minimum number of copies a year. For a textbook, this number could be high, as many as five thousand or more. A publisher also may refuse to authorize a revision for other reasons, for example, if it has acquired another title for the course that has more adoptions. Textbooks in most fields must be revised periodically to continue to be adopted. Consequently, not revising a textbook periodically is likely to kill it, regardless of its merits as a teaching tool.

A self-publisher can revise a textbook or instructional material whenever a revision seems to be needed. In fact, he or she can do so almost continuously, particularly if the textbook or instructional material can be either published on the Internet or printed on demand.

Retaining Copyright

A textbook or instructional material that you author is your property. Amendments to the Copyright Act of 1976 give you and your heirs the exclusive right to exploit the book or material until 70 years after your death. By signing a publishing contract, you transfer ownership of it to the publisher. You lose very little by doing so if the publisher pays you a fair royalty and does an adequate job marketing your book or material. However, based on my own experience and that of many members of the Text and Academic Authors Association, this often does not happen, particularly for a textbook or instructional material that publisher assumes does not have the potential to become a best seller.

If you self-publish a textbook or instructional material, you retain the ownership of copyright. Consequently, you can market it in any way you want, including selling it to a textbook publisher.

Controlling Subsidiary Rights

If someone wants to quote portions of your book or material in a publication, and that use is not permitted by the "fair use" doctrine of the copyright law (see Chapter 10), he or she must get the permission of the copyright owner. Consequently, by transferring copyright to a publisher, the authors essentially loses control over who gets permission to quote from his or her book or otherwise use the material. In fact, as author you lose the ability even to quote extensively from your own work without the publisher's permission. The author receives only a percentage (probably 50 percent) of the permissions fees that are paid. Authors who self-publish a textbook or instructional material retain copyright, and thus retain control over reprint rights as well as other subsidiary rights.

Getting into Print Quickly

It usually takes a minimum of nine months to publish a textbook or instructional material after a publisher has accepted the manuscript for publication. Much of this time is consumed by the manuscript waiting its turn for something to be done to it (e.g., copyediting). By undertaking or outsourcing many of the production tasks, a self-publisher often can shorten this interval.

Making More Money

Your textbook or instructional material may generate more income for you if you self-publish it. Whether it does so depends, of course, on how much it costs you to produce and market it and the number of copies you sell. A number of academic authors who could easily have gotten publishing contracts for their textbooks or instructional materials chose to self-publish because doing so could generate more income.

Directing Marketing and Promotion

Textbooks and instructional materials that a publisher regards as not having the potential to become best sellers are rarely marketed adequately. This means that if you want your book or material to reach as large a segment of its intended audience as possible, you will have to assume an active role in marketing it. However, the publisher's agents responsible for marketing your book or material may not welcome your involvement. Or they may be unable to do what is necessary to market your textbook or instructional material adequately, because the budget available for doing so is inadequate. In fact, the budget may be close to nothing.

If you self-publish a textbook or instructional material, you will have full control over marketing and promoting it. Marketing and promotion involve significant cost in time and money, however. Some possible strategies for these purposes are described in Chapter 11.

Inviting Family Participation

Your involvement in self-publishing may have the potential to benefit one or more members of your family in a number of ways, such as the following.

- Providing spending money for one or more of your high school-age children. Their pay would depend on their responsibilities. As their responsibilities increased, their salary would be expected to also.
- Bringing your relationship with a partner or spouse of one of your children closer to you by working with them on a book project.
- Interesting one or more of your relatives in textbook publishing as a career.

There may well be other indirect benefits from family participation.

Having Pleasure!

Most people who have self-published more than one book or material continued doing so because they enjoy it. As one advocate—Judith Applebaum (1988, p. 151)—stated:

> In these push-button times, the pleasures of physical achievement are reserved mainly for children, but self-publishers, along with a handful of other adults who work with their hands building things they love, are privileged to share the I-made-it-myself elation.

Potential Risks of Self-Publishing

Self-publishing, like all activities, has a "down" as well as an "up" side. That is, you can lose as well as gain from engaging in it. Some of the ways that you could lose by self-publishing textbooks or instructional materials include the following:

- Having to set up a publishing company
- Having to pay substantial costs up front
- Having to spend substantial time on production and marketing
- Having to acquire new knowledge and skills
- Possibly having to engage in activities you do not enjoy
- Possibly not having your self-published textbooks and instructional materials reviewed in professional journals
- Risking possible damage to your professional reputation

The order in which the items are listed is not necessarily related to their importance. Each item is discussed below.

Having to Set Up a Company

Persons who self-publish almost always do so under the name of a company they establish. The company may be structured as a sole proprietorship, partnership, or corporation. It is referred to in the book publishing industry as a small press.

To set up a small press, you will have to make both a time and financial investment. Neither is necessarily huge. Setting up my small press—CODI Publications—required an investment of less than 100 hours and $700. There are step-by-step instructions in Chapter 5 for setting up a small press like mine.

By setting up a small press you would become an entrepreneur. If you considered being a business owner to be incompatible with your self-concept as a college instructor or scholar, you probably would not feel comfortable as a self-publisher. On the other hand, if you regarded becoming an entrepreneur as adding something desirable to your life, then having to become one would make self-publishing even more attractive.

Having to Pay Costs Up Front

For many, cost is the biggest disadvantage of self-publishing. The amount you will have to invest can range from less than $1000 to more than $100,000. At the upper end could be a four-color introductory textbook for a large-enrollment undergraduate course (e.g., introduction to biology that contains many color photographs and anatomical drawings). Consequently, some textbooks tend to be more affordable to self-publish than others. With recent advances in technology, however, more kinds of textbooks are becoming more affordable to self-publish (see Chapter 4).

Having to Spend Time on Publishing Tasks

Producing and marketing a textbook or instructional material will require you to spend time on some production tasks with which you otherwise would not be involved. However, whether or not you self-publish, you will have to spend considerable time on marketing. Unless your textbook or instructional material appears to its publisher to have best-seller potential, it is fairly certain that the publisher will invest little in reaching its audience. If you want readers to become aware of its benefits, you will have to spend time aggressively marketing the book or material.

Having to Acquire New Knowledge and Skills

To produce and market a textbook or instructional material effectively, you will probably have to acquire at least a few new skills, such as creating graphics, negotiating with printers, or writing publicity. While doing so can be time-consuming, it can also be intellectually stimulating. New knowledge and skills can transfer to other contexts, and you can outsource skill areas that you do not enjoy.

Engaging in Activities You May Not Enjoy

If you do not enjoy doing the tasks necessary to produce and market a textbook or instructional material and operate a business, then having to do them would be, for you, a disadvantage of self-publishing. However, you do not have a crystal ball, so you don't know yet what aspects of self-publishing you would and would not enjoy. There is, of course, only one way to determine this, and that is to try. Who knows, you might surprise yourself!

Risking Rejection

Some professional journals have a policy of not reviewing self-published textbooks and instructional materials. If, however, you self-publish under the name of a company you create (see Chapter 5), book review editors may not be aware that your books or materials are self-published and may go ahead and review them. Resources for having your work reviewed are included in the Chapter 11 appendix.

If you self-publish a textbook or instructional material, some of your colleagues and others may assume that it was not of high enough quality to attract a publisher. Their having this belief could damage your professional reputation. One way to minimize this risk is to publish under the name of a company, rather than your own name. Since there are significant numbers of small presses publishing in most fields, very few persons in your field are likely to be aware that your book or material was self-published.

Self-publishing tends to be riskier for non-tenured than for tenured faculty, particularly at institutions that tend to regard themselves as research-focused. If you are on the faculty of such an institution and are not yet tenured, it is crucial that you arrange to have your self-published publication(s) rigorously peer reviewed before going up for tenure.

Some Benefits and Risks of Self-Publishing

Weighing Potential Benefits and Risks

I have candidly described here some possible consequences of self-publishing textbooks and instructional materials. While the risks that I mentioned probably are not the only ones, they do include those that have been cited frequently by self-published authors and in books dealing with self-publishing.

Unfortunately, there is no magic formula that will enable you to predict accurately whether the benefits from self-publishing a particular book or material will outweigh the losses or risks. The best you can do is to weigh, as objectively as you can, the potential benefits and losses to you and to intended readers. And if the scale appears to be heavier on the "Benefits" than on the "Risks" side, seriously consider going ahead, and self-publish!

An Overview of the Self-Publishing Process

To make a real commitment to self-publishing a textbook or instructional material, you would have to be willing to assume (1) that self-publishing the book or material would be academically respectable and (2) that the benefits from self-publishing the book or material would be likely to outweigh the losses. Furthermore, you would have to know how to do or get done each of the essential tasks for publishing successfully.

To assess your ability to do these tasks, you must first understand what they are. An overview of the process for self-publishing a book or material is presented in this chapter, while information on each of the tasks is provided in Chapters 4 through 14.

Successfully self-publishing a book or material requires the following tasks.

- Assess the potential of the book or material for self-publishing.
- Set up a publishing company.
- Author the book or material.
- Decide on the mode of publication—print, electronic, or both.
- Prepare camera-ready and/or electronic copy.
- Index the book or material and prepare the front matter and cover.
- Copyright and register the publication.
- Arrange for printing, binding, and warehousing.
- Do marketing research and promotion.
- Fill orders and maintain financial records.
- Sell subsidiary and reprint rights.

Each area is described briefly below and in greater depth in the chapters that follow.

Organization of This Book in Terms of Self-Publishing Tasks	
Self-Publishing Tasks	*Chapters*
Assessing Project Potential	4
Setting Up a Publishing Company	5
Authoring the Work	6
Deciding on Print or Electronic Publishing	7
Preparing Manuscript	8
Preparing Index, Front Matter, and Cover	9
Obtaining Copyrights and Registrations	10
Printing, Binding, and Warehousing	11
Marketing and Promotion	12
Managing Sales and Record-Keeping	13
Selling Subsidiary and Reprint Rights	14

Assessing the Potential of a Project for Self-Publishing

Some books and materials are more practical than others to self-publish. Factors that determine the practicality of self-publishing a particular text include cost, ease of marketing, and the time investment required. The larger the amount needed up front to publish and market a product, the less practical self-publishing may be. The greater the difficulty in reaching the audience for your project, the less practical self-publishing may be. And the greater the time investment required to publish and market your book or material, the less practical self-publishing may be. These factors and others that can affect the practicality of self-publishing are explored in more detail in Chapter 4.

Setting Up a Publishing Company

Few persons self-publish under their own names. Almost all set up a company for this purpose. They usually set it up either before beginning to create (write) the first book or material they intend to self-publish or immediately after they have begun doing so. Having a company in place at the beginning of the process makes it less likely that deducting expenses will trigger an IRS audit. The procedures for legally setting up a publishing company (i.e., small press) are spelled out in Chapter 5.

Authoring the Book or Material

To self-publish a textbook or instructional material, you first have to write it. Of course, you have to do this even if you're not planning to self-publish. The ways in which you prepare material for publication is likely to be a little different if you're planning to self-publish than if you aren't. These differences are described in Chapter 6, along with a number of suggestions for facilitating the authoring process.

Deciding on the Mode of Publication

You can now publish textbooks and instructional materials electronically as well as on paper. The media options for magnetic and digital publication include audiotapes, CDs, ebooks, and the Internet. There are sites on the Web, for example, from which books and materials can be read or printed after subscribing or paying a fee (usually by credit card). Advantages and disadvantages of print and electronic publishing options for academic self-publishers are discussed in Chapter 7.

Preparing Camera-Ready and Disk Copy

After you create your textbook or instructional material, you or a vendor will have to typeset it and prepare the illustrations for printing. Most typesetting is done by computer, using word-processing and page-layout programs. Illustrations, including photos, are created with or scanned into the computer. After camera-ready copy is generated and the pages are laid out (i.e., the text and illustrations are combined and designed as book pages), the pages are printed out using a laser or inkjet printer or are printed by a photo-offset process.

Preparing pages for electronic publications is usually done similarly, except that the pages are not printed on paper (except as a copy for proofreading). They are published as a computer file, or files, on either a disk (diskette or CD-ROM) or a Web site on the Internet.

Procedures for preparing copy for print and electronic publications are described in Chapter 8.

Indexing and Preparing the Front Matter and Cover

The index for a print publication is prepared after the pages have been laid out and numbered. Several options for preparing an index are described in Chapter 9. The front matter for a print publication is everything up to the start of Chapter 1. It contains some or all of the following elements.

> Half-title page
> Title page
> Copyright page
> Dedication page
> Table of contents
> List of illustrations
> Preface
> Acknowledgments
> Foreword
> Introduction
> Disclaimer

Like the index, most of the front matter usually is prepared after the pages are laid out and numbered, because final page numbers (or folios) are needed for the table of contents and the index. It is desirable, however, that you draft parts of the front matter—particularly the preface and table of contents—before beginning to write. The reason is that these documents set out the purpose, scope, sequence, and rationale for your product, which you should grasp clearly before you begin, even though you probably will revise the preface and table of contents while you are writing your book or material. Considerations when preparing front matter are covered in Chapter 9.

The book cover also is prepared at the beginning, usually by a freelance graphic artist. A photo of the cover often is needed for advance publicity and marketing. The artist also may prepare a dust jacket or an insert cover for a plastic case for a CD-ROM disk or an audiocassette. The text for the back cover of the book or the insert also is drafted. See Chapter 9 for designing covers and case inserts.

All the processes that take place between authoring the manuscript and sending the manuscript to be printed are part of the production phase of publishing. Production tasks include copyediting, preparing illustrations, designing the book, typesetting and composition (page make-up), proofreading, and indexing. Chapters 6-9 focus on these production tasks.

Copyrighting and Registering the Work

Before the copyright page and back cover of a book can be printed, the book must be copyrighted and registered. The book is registered with the Library of Congress and an International Standard Book Number (ISBN) is assigned to it, which is printed on the copyright page. The ISBN (usually in both numerical and barcode format) also is printed on the back cover of the book.

Materials also are copyrighted prior to being published and are registered with the Library of Congress. How-to information about copyrighting and registering books and materials is presented in Chapter 10.

Printing, Binding, and Warehousing

Before a book or material can be distributed and sold, copies must be printed and bound or packaged in some way. The bound or packaged copies are stored until they are sold or otherwise distributed. Options for printing, binding, and warehousing textbooks and instructional materials are presented in Chapter 11.

Marketing

One of the most time-consuming responsibilities that self-publishers must assume is marketing and promotion. No matter how useful a book or material is, it will not have a significant impact if those who could utilize the information it contains are not aware that it exists. This awareness is created through marketing and promotion. Academically respectable strategies that a self-publisher can use to market a textbook or instructional material are described in Chapter 12.

Filling Orders and Maintaining Financial Records

When books or materials are ordered, they must be delivered. And if they are sold rather than given away, adequate financial records must be maintained for tax and other purposes. Options available to academic self-publishers for sales and record keeping are described in Chapter 13.

Selling Subsidiary and Reprint Rights

In addition to distributing your textbook or instructional material yourself, you may give others permission (for a fee) to reproduce and distribute it in whole or part. You may also sell a foreign publisher the right to translate your work into another language. Or you may grow tired of marketing the book yourself and sell the right to reprint and market it to a textbook publisher. Such sales are referred to as

Self-Publishing Process At-A-Glance

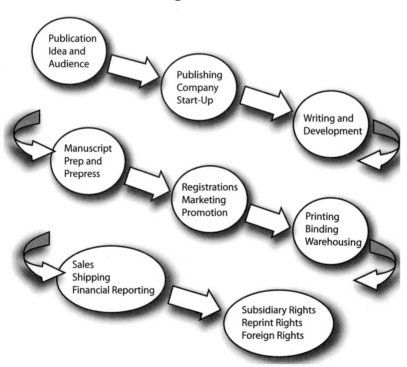

subsidiary rights and reprint rights, the subjects of Chapters 14 and 15. The figure, "Self-Publishing Process At-a-Glance," summarizes the sequence of tasks involved in self-publishing.

It Is Normal to Feel Overwhelmed!

After reading this chapter, you are likely to regard self-publishing a book or material as too time consuming to do. Or you may feel that you lack the ability to acquire the necessary talents. Almost everyone who contemplates self-publishing a book or material initially views the process in this way. In fact, any time you contemplate taking on a long-term project, you are likely to feel overwhelmed. It is like contemplating as a college freshman everything you will have to do during the next eight or so years to earn a Ph.D. While there are some very good reasons not to self-publish a book or material, discussed in Chapter 4, a feeling that the task is too time-consuming or requires talents you do not have and cannot acquire is not usually one of them.

If you consider your book project worthwhile, lacking large blocks of time for writing it should not discourage you. As explained in Chapter 6, short daily blocks of time (e.g., 30 minutes) over a period of a year or so can enable you to complete such a project. A potential benefit of self-publishing is the opportunity to learn and do new things. While you may assume that you lack the ability to acquire some of the skills needed for success in self-publishing, you really won't know unless you try! Some persons allow assumptions or certainties about their abilities to severely limit their lives. One such certainty is the false belief that "you can't teach an old dog new tricks."

Assessing the Practicality of a Project
for Self-Publishing

All types of textbooks and instructional materials can be self-published, including print and non-print course supplements.

Potentially Self-Published Materials	
• Textbook	• Videotape
• Instructor's manual	• Web site or content
• Study guide	• Slide presentation or
• Test item file	photo essay
• Workbook or problem	• Recording
sets	• Teaching guide
• Lab manual	• Lesson plans
• Desk reference	• Distance learning
• Reader or anthology	course
• Audiocassette	• Electronic journal
• CD-ROM	• Ebook

However, some products and projects are more practical to self-publish than others. There are several factors that you should consider when assessing the practicality of self-publishing a particular textbook or instructional material, including the following.

- Your attitude toward self-publishing
- Your attitude toward operating a small business

- The necessary financial investment
- The necessary time investment
- Ease of marketing
- Availability of alternative publishing options

This chapter explores the implications of each for assessing the potential of a book or material for self-publishing.

Your Attitude Toward Self-Publishing

You should take your attitude toward self-publishing into consideration when contemplating self-publishing a textbook or instructional material. If your attitude toward self-publishing is negative, you may want to know why. Possible reasons include the following:

- Gut feeling that it is not academically respectable to self-publish
- Belief that your peers will not value your work if they know it is self-published
- Belief that if your work were worth publishing, a publisher would be willing to publish it

The reasonableness of each "reason" is considered next.

Is It Really Academically Respectable?

While many college faculty question the respectability of self-publishing, they may self-publish without conscious awareness of doing so. They may, for example, distribute copies of convention and conference papers and preprints of articles. They also may distribute handouts they prepare for classes and workshops or make them available on the Internet. All of these are self-published publications! Academics also consider it respectable to self-publish convention papers, preprints of articles, and unpublished research, even if they do not consider this to be self-publishing.

Perhaps the main way that self-publishing a book or material differs from self-publishing a convention paper, a preprint of an article, or an unpublished research report is that recipients are not asked to pay you for copies. If you had a grant enabling you to distribute copies of your work for free, would you self-publish it and regard doing so as academically respectable? The feeling that scholars should not profit financially from what they write probably had its origins during the Middle Ages when almost all scholars were monks. Consequently, they weren't expected to benefit financially from the books they authored.

The reality is that almost all academics profit financially, directly or indirectly, from their writing and other scholarly productivity. Being awarded tenure (and thereby continuing to be employed and receive a salary) is indirect payment for publishing, as is your yearly salary increases. Furthermore, your scholarly productivity influences the number of invitations you are likely to receive to give lectures and conduct workshops for which you receive an honorarium. Consequently, the belief that it is somehow "sinful" to profit financially from your writing and scholarship is not consistent with the reality of the way academia functions.

Finally, some persons in academia believe that being a scholar is not compatible with being an entrepreneur, especially as this relates to authoring textbooks and instructive materials. However, entrepreneurial self-publishing should be perfectly respectable if the textbooks and instructional materials are both of high quality and helpful to intended readers.

Will Your Peers Value a Self-Published Work?

If you publish under the name of a company rather than your name, many (perhaps most) of your peers will not be aware that you are self-publishing. Consequently, self-publishing is not likely to cause your peers to think less well of you, unless, of course, what you self-publish is not of acceptable quality. Unfriendly colleagues who are aware that you are self-publishing may attempt to discredit you or your work, but they might be tempted to do so anyway, unfortunately, even if you were not self-publishing.

Perhaps you believe that your peers will not value any self-published work that they think has not been peer-reviewed. To overcome this concern, you should arrange to have your work thoroughly peer reviewed. Include quotes of complimentary comments from the reviews on the back cover of the book and in promotional materials and packaging. Peer reviewers should have a solid reputation in your field. Ideally, they should include at least one who is almost universally recognized as a leader in the field.

Wouldn't a Publishing Publish It If It Were Worth Publishing?

This belief—that worthwhile projects automatically find publishers—is no longer viable. As outlined in Chapter 3, there are many reasons for self-publishing a work even if a commercial publisher were interested in publishing it. In addition, many worthwhile projects do not get published regardless. Unfortunately, most academic publishers (including even subsidized university presses) avoid publishing unprofitable works. Unless the market for a textbook or instructional material is large enough to be profitable, an author is unlikely to be offered a publishing contract.

Your Attitude Toward Operating a Small Business

When you self-publish books or materials, your municipal, state, and federal governments, including the IRS, regard you as operating a small business. And as such, you will have to abide by all of the laws and regulations that pertain to a small business. You will have become an entrepreneur.

There are at least two reasons that you may resist becoming an entrepreneur. The first, discussed above, is that you might consider becoming an entrepreneur to be incompatible with being an academic. And the second is that you might not have the time available for or interest in becoming an entrepreneur. Is being an entrepreneur compatible with being a college teacher? Specifically, is it appropriate for a teacher to sell the fruits of his or her time and knowledge? Whenever you accept an honorarium for conducting a workshop, you are selling your time and knowledge and, consequently, you are functioning as an entrepreneur. And when you accept a royalty check for a textbook or instructional material, are doing the same thing. While you may not consider such income as coming from a small business, the IRS does. Honorariums, royalties, and income from self-publishing are reported on Schedule C, the same form used for reporting income for all businesses that are not structured as corporations.

Having insufficient time and funding available to operate a small press is, of course, a legitimate reason for not self-publishing. However, you should not reject self-publishing without first determining how much time would be needed and seriously considering whether it would be life enhancing to reorder your priorities in a way that would make it possible for you to do so.

Lack of interest in operating a small press is also a legitimate reason for not self-publishing. However, if you are strongly motivated to have a particular textbook or instructional material published and it seems unlikely to be published in any other way, having to operate as a small publisher may be a small sacrifice for achieving your goal.

Your Ability to Make the Necessary Financial Investment

When you self-publish a textbook or instructional material, you are required to pay its production and marketing expenses up front. As mentioned previously, the amount can vary from less than $1000 or more than $100,000. Factors that can affect your cost of self-publishing a textbook or instructional material include the following:

- Book length and the number and type of illustrations
- Size of the first printing (print run) and trim size of the book (physical dimensions)
- Use of a second color or four-color printing
- Cover(s) and binding(s) used
- Production tasks that are subcontracted
- Warehousing and order fulfillment expenses
- Marketing expenses
- Cost of setting-up your small business

Each factor is discussed in more detail below.

Book Length and Illustrations

The more pages in a book or the more items in an instructional material package, the more expensive production and manufacturing are going to be. Consequently, relatively short books or relatively small sets of materials are likely to be more affordable to self-publish.

Illustrations add to the cost of production in at least two ways. First, they have to be acquired—created or licensed. And second, they have to be prepared for printing and printed. If you create the photographs and drawings, your only out-of-pocket expenses probably will be for materials (assuming you have the necessary equipment). However, if you are unable to create them yourself, you will either have to contract with someone to create them or to purchase reproduction rights from the copyright owner (unless the images are in the public domain).

Regardless of whether you purchase or create illustrations for a book or material, you or a subcontractor will have to prepare them for printing. If they are not already in digital form (e.g., taken with a digital camera), preparation involves scanning them into a computer and having halftones made from them. Creating a halftone of a photograph or drawing converts it into a pattern of tiny dots. In black-and-white illustrations, the size of the dots and the spacing between them determine the darkness of the gray. The larger the dots or the closer the spacing, the darker the gray. The dots in a halftone usually are so small that viewers are unlikely to be aware of them. All photographs and art that is drawn rather than typeset must be converted to halftones before they can be printed. The halftone process is described further in Chapter 8.

The printing of illustrations can add to the cost of producing a textbook or instructional material in three ways. First, it may require the use of a more expensive paper for the entire publication or for pages on which illustrations appear. Second, if a higher quality paper is being used for an inset of illustrations, they may have to be inserted into the books by hand, which would increase cost of printing them. And third, if some pages are in color, they will have to be passed through the press more than once, thereby adding to the cost of printing.

Size of First Printing and Trim Size
In printing a book or material by a photo-offset process, the more copies you print, the less expensive each tends to be. However, the amount of reduction in cost diminishes as the number of copies printed increases. While the cost of printing and binding each book if you print 1,000 copies is likely to be considerably less than if you print 500 copies, the difference in cost between printing 5,500 and 6,000 probably will be very little. The number of copies in a first printing at which savings cease being large enough to justify a larger print one is typically around 3,000.

If a book or material is printed using a photocopy machine, the cost per copy may be almost the same regardless of the number printed. The per-copy cost is higher than for offset printing, however. There are two advantages to printing books and materials by photocopying. The first is to print them only when ordered, and consequently copies do not have to be warehoused. And the second advantage is to make a substantial up-front investment for printing and binding unnecessary. Both advantages are applicable to all short run and print on demand methods of book printing.

The trim size of your book refers to the dimensions of the pages after the book is bound and trimmed. The two most economical trim sizes for books are 5.5 inches by 8.5 inches and 8.5 inches by 11 inches. The first is economical because two pages can be printed on a sheet of 8.5 x 11 paper. And the second is economical because 8.5 x 11 is a standard size that does not need to be trimmed. Other trim sizes frequently used for books are 6 x 9 and 8 x 10. The book you are now reading has a 6 x 9 trim size.

Use of a Second Color or Four-Color Printing

Printing some text (e.g., headings) in a second color in addition to black results in what is called a two-color book. Illustrations also may have "spot color." To print two-color, a page must be printed twice— once with black ink and once with the second (spot color) ink. Having to print pages twice adds to the cost of production.

Using color photographs and multi-color illustrations can add considerably to the cost of printing, because it requires pages to pass through the printer four times. Millions of colors can be simulated by combining the three primary colors plus black in various ways. In addition, four-color printing adds at least two other expenses. First, four plates (rather than just one) for printing each page must be prepared. And second, the images on the four plates for each page must be perfectly aligned.

Cover(s) and Binding(s) Used

The cost of a book's cover and binding are influenced by the design of the cover, the number of colors, the material used for the cover, the dust jacket, and the binding method. Design of the cover can affect the cost of production in two ways. The first is the cost of creating it. According to Dan Poynter (1996), professional book cover designers tend to charge around $1500 for designing and creating the mechanical (i.e., the reproduction quality copy) or disk file for the front, spine, and back of a wrap-around book cover. If, of course, you design and create the mechanical for the cover yourself or have it done by someone who is not a cover designer, the cost may be considerably less.

The number of color plates used to print a book cover ranges from one to four, and four-color covers cost more to print than two-color or one-color ones. In addition, the material on which the cover design is printed affects the cost of production. Hardcover books tend to be more expensive than paperback, but the difference in price is less than most people would suspect.

Hardcover books often have a dust jacket, which can add significantly to the cost of production. A book cover designer may charge a little more to design and create the file for a dust jacket than for a paperback book because of the need to design the front and back flaps that hold the dust jacket in place. Furthermore, the cost of paper, printing, and ink has to be factored in, as well as the cost of wrapping the dust jacket around the book, which may have to be done by hand. You may want to hold down costs by wrapping the dust jackets around the books yourself.

When the pages and cover are bound together, the result is a book. There are a number of ways to bind pages and cover together, and they vary considerably in cost. The least expensive method is stapling. Binding options for textbooks and instructional materials are described in more detail in Chapter 7.

Production Tasks That Are Subcontracted

All textbook and instructional material production tasks can be subcontracted. Few self-publishers do everything themselves, although the more tasks you can do yourself, the less money you will have to invest up front. Production tasks that can be sub-contracted include the following.

- Production editing
- Copyediting
- Preparing illustrations (i.e., photographs and drawings)
- Designing the cover
- Typesetting and laying-out pages
- Preparing page proofs and mechanicals
- Indexing
- Printing and binding

Each of these tasks is described below and in the following chapters.

Organization of This Book in Terms of Production Tasks	
Specific Production Tasks	*Chapters*
Production Editing and Copyediting	6, 8
Preparing Illustrations and Photographs	6, 8
Cover and Book Design	7, 8
Typesetting and Page Layout	6, 8
Preparing Page Proofs and Mechanicals	8
Indexing	9
Printing and Binding	7

It is possible to retain a freelance production editor, sometimes called a packager, to oversee the entire production process. This person serves as your agent for subcontracting and monitoring production tasks. Of course, retaining someone to oversee the production process will add to the cost of production. If minimizing your time investment is more important to you than minimizing your financial investment, however, then retaining an experienced production editor is certainly worth considering seriously.

It is also important to copyedit a book or material manuscript for grammatical, stylistic, and spelling errors and for clarity before it is typeset and printed. While some authors are better able than others to edit their writings, few (if any) are so good at doing so that they can dispense with a good copyeditor. Unless you have a colleague, family member, or friend who is both competent at copyediting and willing to conscientiously copyedit a book-length manuscript, you will have to contract with someone to do it. Professional copyeditors typically earn between $2.00 and $4.00 per page.

If there are illustrations you need that you cannot create yourself nor obtain permission to reproduce from books, journals, or other sources, you will have to retain a graphic artist and/or a photographer to create them. Doing so can be expensive. Even if your ability as an artist is quite limited, you may still be able to create some of the illustrations that you need yourself. Your word processing program or other software will generate or draw almost any type of table or graph. Some programs will convert numbers in designated rows and columns from a spreadsheet into a graph. No artistic ability is needed to draw graphs of this kind. Incidentally, if you hired a graphic artist, he or she probably would draw your graphs using the same kind of software.

Someone with limited artistic ability also can create illustrations other than graphs. Software exists that will almost automatically draw flow charts and matrices. In addition, there is software available that enables you to modify existing scanned illustrations to meet your needs. Of course, if the use of such an illustration or portion of it is not defined as "fair use," you will have to get permission from the copyright owner to use it (see Chapter 10).

Finally, if you have available a 35mm or digital camera, you may be able to produce some of the photographs that you need for illustrations, depending on your skill as a photographer. Prints and slides, as well as digital files, can be used for this purpose. It is also possible to produce black-and-white illustrations from color photographs.

Most textbook publishers use freelancers to design and produce the files for their book covers, dust jackets, and inserts for containers for CDs and audiocassettes. These are now almost always typeset and laid out with a computer. The graphic elements in them are either computer-generated or scanned from photographs or drawings. Whether you attempt to produce your book's cover, dust jacket, or case insert yourself, you will need to make decisions about what to use. Look at the covers of other books in your market of the same trim size as yours, and use cover designs that appeal to you as models. One strategy for locating ideas for covers is to browse in a college or trade bookstore. Cover design is discussed further in Chapter 7.

Typesetting and laying out pages are done on a computer. If the page design is relatively straightforward, it can be done with a word-processing program or a publishing program such as QuarkXPress, InDesign, or the older Page Maker. Note, however, that you may need to take a course to learn how to use these programs effectively. Sometimes you can typeset and lay out pages while you are drafting the manuscript, and there are guidelines for this in Chapters 6 and 8.

If you contract to have pages typeset and laid out, you will be provided with galleys, page proofs, and an art and photo manuscript. If you typeset and lay out pages yourself, you can print page proofs on a laser or ink jet printer. However, if your manuscript contains photographs and your home printer is not capable of printing at least 1,400 dpi (dots per inch), you would have to arrange to have those pages printed by a service bureau. On the other hand, if your book has no illustrations or its illustrations are typeset, printing at 720 dpi or higher is usually adequate.

Another common production task that is outsourced in indexing. A good index is crucial for a textbook. You can have your index prepared by a freelance indexer or you can do it yourself. Professional freelance indexers charge between 50 cents and a dollar per item. Unless you can locate an indexer who is familiar with both your field and the topics your book covers, you would be wise prepare the index yourself. Guidelines for indexing a textbook are presented in Chapter 9.

Finally, printing and binding are among the few tasks that are impractical to try to do yourself. Because the cost can vary considerably, get at least three estimates from different book printers. You can solicit bids from many printers simultaneously by using automated "Request for Quote" (RFQ) forms online. Chapter 7 contains a discussion of options for printing and binding.

Finding Competent Freelance Production Help

Few persons, if any, can copyedit their writing as well as a competent copyeditor (Michener, 1992). Consequently, few books would be considered as well written if a competent copyeditor had not improved the writing in them. During the past 25 years (during which I have had many books published), I have attempted to correct writing problems in a manuscript before submitting it. And in almost every instance, changes in a manuscript that a copyeditor suggested improved the writing. I would never consider self-publishing a book manuscript before having it competently copyedited!

Most persons who copyedit manuscripts for textbooks are freelancers, and there are at least three ways to go about finding one. One would be to ask other academic self-publishers for recommendations. A second would be to ask staff from your University Press (or possibly even another University Press) for recommendations. And a third would be to ask other recent textbook authors at your institution for recommendations of freelance copyeditors with whom they were satisfied. Finally, many freelancers in all areas of book production advertise on the Internet.

Online Resources for Getting Production Help

Writing Network: http://www.writingnetwork.com
Editorial Freelancers Association: http://www.the-efa.org
Freelance illustrators and other services at Elance Online: http://www.elance.com
Book-Editing Associates: http://www.book-editing.com
Small Publishers, Artists, and Writers Network (SPAWN): http://www.spawn.org
Book cover designers: http://www.brennerbooks.com/coverdesigners

The same is true for cover designers, graphic artists, and book illustrators. It is important to have the front, back, and spine of the cover for a paperback textbook designed professionally, unless you have particular competence to do this yourself, especially if you do not want the book to appear to have been self-published. The book cover designer both designs the cover and prepares the files for printing it. In addition, most textbooks require some figures other than photographs. These figures range in complexity from line drawings to grayscale or color illustrations (e.g., anatomical drawings). Be aware that preparing grayscale and color illustrations can be very expensive!

There are several possible sources for such artists. One is to seek recommendations from other self-publishers, particularly those whose books contain illustrations that are similar to those you will need and are done well. A second is recommendations from the graphic service department at or near your university. A graphic artist employed by the institution may be interested in doing some figures for you on the side as a moonlighting project. A third possibility is to recruit a student from a high school or college who already has adequate skills as a graphic artist for your purposes.

Warehousing and Order Fulfillment Expenses

After your book or material has been produced and manufactured, the copies will be delivered to you. If you choose not store them in your home or office, you probably will have to pay to have them warehoused. If you print copies of your product on demand or if you publish via the

Internet, you will not have warehousing expenses. Nor will you have them if you print relatively small numbers of copies (e.g., 500 at a time). Of course, the amount you save on warehousing by printing on demand or having small print runs may be offset by having to pay significantly more per copy for printing and binding.

There are expenses associated with order fulfillment whether or not you pay someone to do it. These expenses include office supplies, shipping containers, and postage (or UPS charges). Some publishers include shipping charges (i.e., postage and handling) in the price of their books, and others treat them as a separate item. An overview of procedures that many self-publishers use for warehousing and filling orders is given in Chapter 12.

Marketing Expenses

Persons who can benefit from your textbook or instructional material will be unable to do so unless they are aware that it exists. Marketing is the process through which potential consumers become aware that your product is available. A number of approaches traditionally have been used—singly or in combination—for marketing textbooks and instructional materials. While all methods require a financial investment, some require considerably more than others. Some conventional marketing strategies for textbooks and instructional materials are described in Chapter 11.

Your Ability to Make the Necessary Time Investment

In addition to spending time operating a small business, an author who self-publishes will almost always have to invest more time in his or her book project. The amount of additional time that an author will have to invest is likely to be influenced by a number of factors, including the nature of the project, the production tasks that are subcontracted, the marketing plan, and the approach used for filling orders. How can these factors affect the time investment needed to self-publish a particular book or material?

Not all textbooks and instructional materials require the same level of investment to self-publish. Some are more affordable than others. The time investment required to self-publish a book or material ranges, for example, from fewer than 100 hours to thousands of hours.

However, the more production tasks you subcontract, the less time you will need to invest to self-publish. The specific production tasks you subcontract also will affect time, because some tasks tend to be more time-consuming than others.

The better defined your market is for a particular book or material, the easier it will be to reach, and consequently the less time you will need to spend alerting potential consumers to its availability. The market for a speech pathology textbook, for example, is more narrowly defined (and therefore easier to reach) than the market for this book, which includes college instructors in all subject areas. While there are only about 225 colleges and universities in the United States that have speech pathology training programs, someone interested in self-publishing textbooks or instructional materials could be in any department of any of the more than 4,000 institutions of higher learning in this country.

Finally, if you fill orders yourself, your time investment is likely to be considerably greater than if you have somebody else do it. There are firms that offer sales and distribution to self-publishers.

Ease of Marketing and Availability of Publishing Alternatives

The audience for some educational books and materials is more clearly defined and more easily communicated with than others. The better defined and more easily accessed the audience for a particular book or material is, the more practical it tends to be to self-publish for that audience.

Ease of marketing should be given considerable weight when deciding whether to self-publish. It is perhaps the first thing you should consider when making this decision. If you are unable or unwilling to do what is necessary to adequately market a book or material to a large segment of its potential audience, you probably would be unwise to self-publish, unless your goal is merely to see your work in print. If marketing proves difficult or too time-consuming, you could hire a marketing manager or publicist to assist you.

Because most textbook publishers are concerned with pro-fitability, self-publishing is the only viable option for publishing many potentially helpful—even essential—textbooks and instructional materials with only modest projections of sales. Of course, being unable to document an adequate-size market to be profitable does not necessarily mean that there is no such market. Sometimes the market for a book for which an author is unable to attract a publisher is later found to be sufficiently large after the book is self-published. Reprint rights for self-published textbooks have been purchased by major textbook publishers who rejected them initially. One such book in my field (speech-language pathology) was purchased from a self-publisher in the late 1930s and has been revised periodically since then. In any event, alternative publishing options are a factor in assessing the potential of a textbook or instructional project for self-publishing.

In conclusion, then—to summarize—your decision to self-publishing a particular work must rest on the following four key factors.

Four Key Factors to Consider in Deciding to Self-Publish

- Your ability to provide a peer-reviewed, academically respectable, scholarly, or pedagogically sound work.
- Your ability, time, and money to invest in and manage a small business enterprise.
- Your product's needs and costs in terms of editorial, production, manufacturing, and fulfillment services.
- Your ability to bring your product to your intended audience through marketing and sales.

Setting Up Your Publishing Company

Almost all self-publishers find it advantageous to set up a publishing company. There are at least two reasons. First, it facilitates keeping records for tax and other purposes and benefiting from business-related tax deductions. And second, it tends to make the fact that your books or materials are self-published less obvious than it would be otherwise. If your publications are printed and bound (or packaged) in a manner similar to those of other publishers, few persons will be aware that they were self-published.

This chapter assumes that your small press will be publishing only textbooks or instructional materials that you author, that your company will be housed in your home, and that you will have no full-time employees. Those who do tasks for you will be functioning as independent contractors. Tasks you will have to do to set up a small press including the following.

- Select a business structure.
- Obtain business licenses and permits.
- Select a name for the company and register it.
- Rent a post office box.
- Open a business checking account and arrange for merchant card service.
- Set up a bookkeeping system.
- Register a domain name and set up a Web site.
- Secure an "800 number" for ordering.
- Have stationery printed.
- Purchase equipment and supplies.
- Obtain ISBNs for your company's publications.

41

- Obtain copyright forms.
- Apply for the Library of Congress Pre-Assigned Control Number and Cataloging in Publication Number.
- Arrange for copyediting.
- Select a firm to print and bind your publication.

The procedures for accomplishing each of these tasks are summarized below. Selected online resources for accomplishing these tasks are listed in the chapter appendix.

Select a Business Structure

Three possible business structures can be utilized for a small press—a sole proprietorship, a partnership, or a corporation. Each has advantages and disadvantages. The sole proprietorship is the type used by most academic self-publishers. What you earn you get to keep and what you owe is your responsibility to pay. You file a Schedule C with your federal income tax return in which you report income and expenses. Your small press will function as a sole proprietorship if you do not set it up as a partnership or corporation. It tends to be less expensive to set up a business as a sole proprietorship than as a partnership or corporation. The main disadvantage is that you are responsible for all debts. If, for example, you are sued because of something someone objects to in your textbook or instructional material, and you lose, then you will be responsible for paying legal fees and any damages assessed by the court, even if the amount exceeds the value of your company. A worst-case scenario would be your having to sell your home and liquidate your other assets to pay them or declare bankruptcy.

With regard to both taxes and liability responsibilities, a partnership is essentially the same as a sole proprietorship. What the partners earn they get to keep, and what they owe is their responsibility to pay. While, having a partner (or partners) reduces your financial liability in the event of a worst-case scenario, it also makes you responsible for any business-related debts that a partner incurs. Persons who self-publish a textbook they co-author will be regarded by the IRS and other government agencies as a partnership—unless the small press they set up to publish it was as either a sole proprietorship or corporation. Partnerships have other legal ramifications, and consequently you would be wise to consult an attorney before entering into one.

A corporation differs from a sole proprietorship and a partnership in that it exists as an entity independent of the person or persons who establish it. While you do not get to keep what the corporation earns, it can compensate you in various ways (e.g., contribute to your retirement account or pay you a consulting fee). The law gives corporations the status of "persons." They can, for example, be sued and convicted of crimes. The money a corporation earns belongs to its stockholders but its debts are almost always its responsibility alone. Consequently, one advantage of a corporate structure is that any debt is limited to the assets of the business. Your home probably would not be at risk if the assets of the corporation were not adequate to pay debts. A corporation, incidentally, does not have to be a business with employees. In some states, it can be a one-person business. Having a corporate structure has a number of tax and legal implications. Consequently, you'd be wise to consult a CPA and an attorney if you were considering this structure for your company.

Obtain Business Licenses and Permits

As a self-publisher you are operating a small business. Consequently, you will have to apply for any licenses and permits that are required to operate a small business. The specific licenses and permits that you must acquire vary somewhat from municipality to municipality as well as from state to state.

If your state has a sales tax and you sell textbooks or instructional materials to persons in your state on a retail basis, you must collect sales tax and pay those amounts to the state. Customers in other states would not pay your state's sales tax, however. Also, you do not collect sales taxes on books you sell to resellers (e.g., college bookstores) in any state, nor on books you sell to "exempt" nonprofit or public institutions in your state. The theory about resellers is that a sales tax should not be paid on an item more than once, and that the retailer is responsible for collecting it. To avoid being legally responsible for sales taxes for sales to retailers, you will probably have to apply for a reseller's license or permit. Having such a license or permit may also enable you to avoid having to pay a sales tax on printing and binding copies of your book or material if it is done in your state.

A valuable resource for information about licenses and permits as well as other aspects of setting up a small business is

SCORE, the Small Business Administration's volunteer network. SCORE—which stands for "Service Corps of Retired Executives"— consists of retired men and women who are both willing and able to provide such information. There is no charge for this service. SCORE is administered by the U.S. Small Business Administration (SBA), which should be listed in your telephone book. See also the chapter appendix.

Name Your Company and Register It

While you can name your publishing company almost anything that you wish, there are some names you would probably be wise to avoid. One would be a name that is already being used by another publishing company. One source you can consult to determine if a name you are considering is already being used is *Books in Print*. Using the same name as another publisher is not illegal unless the name is a registered trademark, but doing so can lead to confusion and, consequently, is not desirable. You can conduct an online company name search for under $20.

Another type of name to avoid is a registered trademark for another product, particularly a well known one. You could be sued for calling your company the "McDonald Publishing Company" if your name is not McDonald. Actually, it is not a particularly good idea to include your name in the company name (e.g., Franklin Silverman Enterprises). Doing so makes it obvious to reviewers and potential customers that the book or material was self-published. If they have a bias against self-published works, knowing this could make them less likely to review it or buy it. The name you select should be both academically respectable and relatively easy to pronounce and spell. And if you are going to have a logo, the name should be one for which a logo can be created that will reinforce the academically respectable image of your company. It's crucial that your company and its publications be viewed in this way to establish your professional reputation as a self-publisher.

You will have to file a "fictitious name" statement, also known as a "dba" ("doing business as…"). The public has a right to know the names of people doing business under a company name. In some states you register your company name by filing a dba document or placing a legal notice in a local daily or weekly newspaper.

Rent a Post Office Box

Your company must, of course, have a mailing address for ordering and payment. While you can use your home's street address, most self-publishers prefer to use a post office box. Small ones (5 x 5.5 inches) could be rented for about $90 a year when this chapter was written, or you may want a larger one (11 x 5.5 inches) for $160 per year. Five sizes of post office box usually are available. Some commercial textbook publishers, incidentally, also use P.O. boxes for these purposes.

There are several reasons that self-publishers find it advantageous to use a P.O. box rather than their street address for a company address. One is security. A post office box tends to be more secure than a home mailbox, particularly for checks. A second advantage of P.O. boxes is size. While home mailboxes have a finite capacity, P.O. boxes do not. If the amount of mail addressed to your P.O. box exceeds its capacity, a note is placed in your box alerting you to retrieve excess mail by presenting the note to a clerk.

A third advantage of using a P.O. box for your company's mailing address is that doing so will help you to maintain your privacy. People will not be coming to your home uninvited because they assume it is a business or want to share with you their reactions to your publications. You might welcome such feedback, but at an appropriate time and place. A fourth possible advantage of using a P.O. box is that your company's mailing address will not be affected by your change of residence, so long as picking up your mail at the same post office is convenient.

Generate Working Capital

If you self-publish, you will need working capital to set up your company and to produce and market your textbook or instructional material. The amount needed can range from less than $1,000 to more than $100,000. For a 200 page 5.5-inch by 8.5-inch book, printed in one color (black ink), that has only a few illustrations, a four-color wraparound cover, and a first printing of 3,000 copies, the amount of working capital needed is likely to be at least between $12,000 and $16,000 (Poynter, 2002). It may be possible to secure the working capital you need to self-publish from one or more of the following sources:

- Your financial resources
- A personal or business loan
- A grant
- A prepublication special offer
- Royalty financing

The pros and cons of each are considered below.

Your Financial Resources

Most self-publishers use their own money for working capital (Poynter, 2002). If the money you have available for self-publishing is limited, you may still be able to fund it by doing almost all of the prepress production tasks yourself, by having a relatively small first printing, or by printing on demand.

A Personal or Business Loan

Sources from which self-publishers have borrowed working capital include family or friends. Another source is signature loans from banks. Self-publishers often are more successful in getting such a loan when the reason they give for needing it is something other than publishing—e.g., a vacation. It does not seen too far-fetched to view time spent on self-publishing as a vacation from normal activities! You may be able to establish a line of credit at your bank at a reasonable interest rate, especially if you can put up collateral. Some self-publishers have gotten started with money from a second mortgage or an equity loan.

Another source from which self-publishers borrow working capital is credit card companies. You pay for printing, binding, and possibly other publishing and marketing expenses using a credit card. Credit card companies that specialize in small businesses, such as American Express, allow you to borrow low-interest cash on your card as well. The advantage is that you do not have to apply for a loan or put up collateral. The main disadvantage is that the interest rate is likely to be higher than that for a personal loan from a bank. For a business loan from you bank or other institution, you must provide supporting documents—such as credit reports, profit-and-loss statement, and projected 3-year cash flow spreadsheets—to encourage them to invest in you and your business.

One source of working capital is a business loan through the offices of the Small Business Administration. In most states, the SBA has a microloan program designed especially to help part-time or home-based businesses. Microloans are for up to $35,000. It is important to understand that the SBA does not give loans but prequalifies you to receive secured loans from local private microlenders. If you receive an SBA "loan," you likely will have up to 10 years to repay it. If your goal is to finance a publishing enterprise, SBA resources should be first on your list.

A Grant

For many academic self-publishers, having a business is secondary. You may find that funding is available from your department or institution to support educational or scholarly publication projects. Support may be indirect as well as direct. Examples include sabbatical and released time funding as well as summer faculty and research grants. Some private foundations offer grants for worthwhile publishing projects in various subject areas. There are databases you can use to identify foundations that may as part of their mission provide support for scholars in your field.

A Prepublication Special Offer

Three or four months before your textbook or material is ready to be printed, you mail a flyer or postcard to persons who might be interested in it and offer a special reduced price for prepublication orders. You may offer a discount of 10 to 50 percent up to a certain date. You may want to indicate that you will not cash checks or submit charges for credit card purchases until the book is shipped. Specify a realistic shipping date. Depending on the size of your sample, the response to such a mailing can be helpful when deciding an optimal size for a first printing. However, direct mailings typically bring returns of only 1 or 2 percent.

Royalty Financing

An investor can lend you money for self-publishing a book or material in exchange for a royalty on every copy sold. Consequently, if no copies are sold, you don't have to pay the investor anything. Another nice feature of this form of financing is that you don't have to pay anything on the "loan" until money comes in from sales. It is a good idea to limit the term of the agreement to the first printing. Any contract you must sign to receive such financing should be checked by your attorney.

You may also be able to interest an individual, business, charitable organization, venture capitalist, or some other institution in financing your publishing project in whole or in part prior to publication in exchange for copies. The sponsor typically has a say about the project content. What the sponsor may get out of the deal is a premium to distribute to its customers or members or a product that advances one or more of the sponsor's objectives.

Open a Business Checking Account and Arrange Card Service

You must be able to document adequately your publishing-related income and expenses for the IRS and possibly other municipal, state, and federal government agencies. You need such documentation, for example, to complete Schedule C of your federal income tax return, assuming that your business structure is a sole proprietorship. One way to keep track of and document both income and expenses is to open a business checking account. You use the account to pay publication-related expenses and deposit in it the income you receive from the sale of your textbooks or instructional materials. It is important to keep your business financial transactions separate from personal ones in any case.

Your bank can also help you establish a merchant card service so that your customers can purchase your works using their credit cards. Both the bank and each credit card company charge a fee for this service, usually a small-percentage transaction fee, whether you process sales online or use a mechanical device for transmitting credit card data. E-commerce Web hosts also can arrange for merchant card service and the processing of credit card sales, for example, through PayPal.

Set Up a Bookkeeping System

All businesses require an accounting system. While it can be helpful to consult an accountant when setting one up, a software program that assumes no previous accounting knowledge—such as QuickBooks—may be adequate for the purpose. These programs track your customers, sales, sales taxes (if any), accounts receivable, inventory, expenses by category, and other data, which are displayed in spread sheets and graphs. You can create invoices and packing slips with this software and even arrange shipping and banking. Some programs also will automatically complete and print Schedule C of your federal income tax return, as well as the comparable schedule for your state income tax return, where applicable. You may need to take a course to learn to use accounting programs properly. However, even if you keep your own books, it is advisable to consult a tax accountant. Freelance bookkeepers can be found locally if you do not have the time to perform this business task and can afford professional services.

Set Up a Web Site

It has become essential for a publisher—even a small one—to have a domain name and a home page on the Web. Your Web site can be used for both promoting and ordering your books and materials, as well as for other purposes. A site for your textbook could support student research of assignments by providing extra content or links to Web sites that deal with chapter topics. You could license or syndicate your site to instructors who adopt your textbook. Students could complete assignments online and email them to their instructors.

In addition to promoting your publications on your own Web site, you will want to arrange to promote and sell your products on other Web sites, particularly online bookstores such as Barnes & Noble and Amazon.com. You may also want to arrange to link and from other Web sites related to your content. You will get the best results from a professional-looking Web site serviced by a reliable Web host, which may take some research and investment. Chapter 11 has more information about marketing online.

Secure Toll-Free Numbers for Ordering

To encourage ordering by phone or fax and paying by credit card, it would be desirable for your business to have toll-free numbers. A toll-free number could rink on a phone at your home or at an order-taking service. A toll-free fax could provide a virtual fax you receive via your company's email address. In addition to providing a professional image for your company, an answering service may be accessible for order taking almost every day and time of day. You are charged a small monthly or annual service fee for toll-free numbers, plus an amount for each incoming call.

Have Business Stationery Printed

You are going to want to have company letterhead, envelopes, mailing labels, and business cards printed, or you may try to do this yourself using desktop publishing software. Both the printing and paper you use should convey a dignified (academically respectable) image. You may be able to design the letterhead so that it can also be used for invoices if you do not plan to print them with your accounting program.

When you have your stationary printed, you may also want to have self-inking rubber stamps made. For example, one that prints "Media Rate" in large letters could be used on envelopes, if which you ship books via the cheapest U.S. mail rate. You would not use this stamp if you ship via other delivery services, such as FedEx or UPS, however. Another stamp could print "Pay to the Order of…(your bank) " or "For Deposit Only…(your business account)." You would use the latter stamp for endorsing checks before depositing them, which helps to reinforce your company's image as a business.

You also will need to research the best kind of packaging or mailers for your book or material and buy in some quantity if you are planning to fill orders yourself. The trim size of the book and the thickness of the spine will determine the size of the mailer for single-copy sales. You should choose mailers that will minimize any possible damage to your books in transit or in packing and unpacking, because people will not buy damaged books, and wholesalers and retailers will insist on returning any products that arrive in less than perfect condition. Review the catalogs of business materials suppliers for pricing information on packaging.

Purchase Equipment and Supplies

You will need a computer with an inkjet or laser printer. While one that prints 300 dots per inch (dpi) will be usable for text and line drawings, one that prints 600 or more dpi will yield pages that more closely approximate professionally typeset pages. For illustrations other than plain line drawings, a printer capable of producing at least 1200 dpi is desirable.

If you are not outsourcing production, the software you will need to create camera-ready copy or computer files from which pages can be typeset is either a word processing program that has page layout capabilities (e.g., Microsoft Word) or a page layout program (e.g.,

InDesign, Quark Xpress, Aldus PageMaker, or others). In addition, if you are planning to produce your own illustrations, you probably will need at least one art and photograph manipulation program (e.g., Adobe Photoshop) and possibly also a scanner. Other computer hardware and software you will need include a high-speed modem or DSL Connection, strong virus protection, and business management software of some kind.

You also may need to purchase office furniture, if you don't already have it, and the usual office equipment and supplies. Incidentally, all of the equipment and supplies you purchase to enable you to self-publish is tax deductible so long as they are used solely for this purpose. In addition, a portion of your home expenses, including mortgage and utilities, can be deducted for the space you use exclusively for conducting your business. You would be advised to check with an accountant.

Obtain ISBNs

The book industry uses ISBNs (International Standard Book Numbers) to identify books uniquely for ordering and other purposes. It is a ten-digit number that identifies both the publisher and the book title. Brick-and-mortar and online bookstores will not stock books that do not have an ISBN clearly printed on the back cover and copyright page. You purchase ISBNs from R.R. Bowker, 630 Central Ave., New Providence, NJ 07974, and this can be done online. For a handling fee of $225, you will be assigned an ISBN identifying prefix for your company and a block of ten ISBN numbers. You will use each number once and only once for each book or material you publish and each revised edition, if any. Different printings of the same book—e.g., hardback and paperback—each also receive a unique ISBN.

You activate a set of ISBN numbers by registering a book online at the Bowker Web site or by completing and submitting an Advanced Book Information (ABI) form, available from Bowker, once you have published three or more titles. By submitting your registration, you get your book listed in *Books in Print* at no charge. Other directory listings are desirable as well.

In addition to printing an ISBN in your book, you will have to order an EAN Bookland bar code for the back cover. The bar code includes the ISBN and, optionally, the price of the book in the form of electronically scannable printed bars, as on the back cover of this book. Know what your distributors and sellers prefer, however. In some cases, having the price on the book is not desirable, while in other cases having the price in different currencies (such as US and Canadian) is preferred.

Obtain Copyright Forms

You should formally copyright your textbook or academic materials. While you have some copyright protection without formally registering your work, you can get significantly more protection by doing so. The registration process consists of completing a form after your book is in print, paying a $30 fee, and submitting these along with two copies of the publication to the Library of Congress, U.S. Copyright Office, 101 Independence Ave. S.E., Washington, D.C. 20559-6000 (www.copyright.gov). You order the form (Form TX) in advance of publication from the Registrar of Copyrights, or download it from U.S. Copyright Office web site. The publication you submit is likely to be catalogued as a part of the permanent collection of the Library of Congress, though this often takes considerable time.

Apply for a PCN and CIP Data

If your publication is a book of more than 50 pages and is likely to be purchased by libraries (which would be the case for almost all textbooks), you should apply for a Library of Congress Pre-Assigned Control Number (PCN). There is no charge for this number, which is printed on the copyright page of your book. The number you are assigned is called the LCCN (Library of Congress Control Number), which is reserved for self-published books and books by authors or publishers with fewer than three titles in print.

You also will need Cataloging in Publication (CIP) data or Publisher's Cataloging in Publication (PCIP) data. CIP data, in a form that one finds on cards in a library's card catalog, is provided by librarians at the Library of Congress, who catalog your book based on its contents. PCIP data is very similar to CIP data except that it is provided by freelance librarians as a service to publishers. This service is needed, for example, by publishers with fewer than three titles in print. You can contract for PCIP services for as little as $30 per title to as much as $150. See the Chapter 10 appendix for online sources of help with copyrighting and registering a self-published work.

Arrange for Copyediting

While you can certainly improve your writing by carefully editing what you write, and by running your spell-check utility, there is a limit to how far you can do so yourself. Sentences and paragraphs that seem clear to you may not be clear—or as clear as they could be—to a reader. In addition, there may be reference errors—e.g., the year listed for a paper you cited in the narrative and in the references may be different, or you may have forgotten to include the reference for a paper you cited. And, of course, it is likely you failed to detect at least a few spelling and grammatical errors. For these reasons and possibly others, you should arrange for someone to copyedit your manuscript before it is formatted or typeset for printing. Further, you would be wise to have your work copyedited by a professional or an experienced manuscript editor.

Arrange for Printing and Binding

Your manufacturer can be either a local printer or a book maker. If you are printing 500 or more copies at a time, the cost per copy is likely to be less if you use a book manufacturer, especially if your book will be case bound or a paperback. A local printer is likely to have to subcontract for these types of bindings. Book manufacturers are listed in directories, such as *The Literary Marketplace*, available both online and in the Reference section of most college and municipal libraries.

The cost of printing and binding a particular number of books or materials can vary considerably. Consequently, it is important to get written quotes or bids from at least three or four printers or book manufacturers. Choose printers that customarily work with small presses. Also get quotes or bids for different size print runs to inform your printing decisions. You also can request printing quotes online by filling out form fields specifying what you are looking for (e.g., trim size, page count, paper type and weight, cover specs, number of halftones, and type of binding). You will receive competitive bids from a wide variety of printers.

In conclusion, here is a checklist for becoming a self-publisher. In addition, the chapter appendix offers some sources of help for setting up your small press, and you will find more information on sales in Chapter 11.

Becoming a Self-Publisher: A Checklist

A. BUSINESS	❏ Select a business structure.
	❏ Obtain business licenses and permits.
	❏ Select a company name and file a DBA.
	❏ Set up and equip an office.
B. COMMUNICATION	❏ Rent a post office box.
	❏ Have business stationery printed.
	❏ Set up a Web site.
C. FINANCE	❏ Open a business checking account.
	❏ Set up a bookkeeping system.
	❏ Generate working capital.
D. PUBLISHING	❏ Obtain ISBNs, copyright forms, and publisher listings.
	❏ Obtain LOC control catalog numbers.
	❏ Arrange reviewing, copyediting, indexing, and design.
	❏ Contract for printing and binding or manufacturing.
E. SALES	❏ Arrange for publicity, advertising, and promotion.
	❏ Secure an 800 number for ordering.
	❏ Arrange for credit card purchasing.
	❏ Develop relationships with wholesalers and retailers.

Online Resources for Setting Up Your Publishing Company

Information about Starting a Small Business

Small Business Administration (SBA): http://sba.gov (See especially the explanation of business structures.)
US Business Advisor (for home-based businesses, sponsored by SBA): http://www.business.gov
Service Core of Retired Executives (SCORE): http://www.score.org
United States Postal Service: http://www.usps.com (find info about box rentals at your local PO and see the "Grow Your Business" section.)
Starting and Growing a Small Business: http://www.entrepreneur.com
Toll-free products and services: http://www.accessline.biz; www.messagingservice.com Virtual fax: www.protus.com/services/vf.com

Information about the Book Publishing Business

Dan Poynter on self-publishing: http://www.parapublishing.com
Self-Publishing for Profit: http://www.powerhomebiz.com/vol92/selfpublishing/
Useful articles on self-publishing: http://desktoppub.about.com/cs/selfpublishing/
Directory of book publishing resources: http://www.bookzonepro.com/resources/
Books on book publishing: http://www.wiseowlbooks.com/publish/bestbooks.html
Tom and Marilyn Ross on self-publishing: http://www.communicationcreativity.com

Information about Licenses and Registrations

Books in Print: http://www.booksinprint.com
Bowker's: http://www.bowker.com
ISBNs: http://www.isbn.org
Library of Congress Cataloging in Publication Program: http://cip.loc.gov/cip
Library of Congress Preassigned Control Number Program: http://pcn.loc.gov/pcn
(See especially http://pcn.loc.gov/pcn/pcnfaq.html.)

Directory for Information on Sales Taxes, by State: http://www.
    taxsites.com/state.html
U.S. Copyright Office: http://www.loc.gov/copyright (For Form TX,
    see http://www.loc.gov/copyright/forms.)
EAN Bookland Bar Codes: http://www.mecsw.com/specs/
    bookland.html

Information about Banking and Merchant Card Services

American Express: http://www.americanexpress.com (Click on
    "OPEN: The Small Business Network.")
Information about merchant accounts: http://www.
    monstermerchantaccount.com
Card Service International: http://www.cardservice.com
Bank Card USA: http://www.bankcardusa.com

Information about Financing a Small Business

Small Business Administration Microloans: http://sba.gov/
    financing/sbaloan/microloans.htm
Foundation Center: http://fdcenter.org
Foundation Grants to Individuals: http://gtionline@fdcenter.org
    ($9.95/mo.)
Council on Foundations: http://www.cof.org
Information about Grants and Grant Writing: http://www.
    proposalwriter.com/small.html
Entrepreneur.com: http://www.entrepreneur.com/Your_Business/
    (See especially the article on royalty financing.)

Information about Publishing Software

Book publishing software: http://www.bookpublishingsoftware.com
Desktop Publishing (with free templates, tutorials, and reviews):
    http://www.desktoppublishing.com
Publishers' Assistant: http://www.pubassist.com
PUB123: http://www.adams-blake.com/pub123/pub123demo.html
QuickBooks: http://www.quickbooks.com
Adobe InDesign: http://www.adobe.com/products/indesign/main.
    html
Adobe Page Maker: http://www.adobe.com/products/pagemaker/
    main.html
Quark Xpress: http://www.quark.com

Adobe Photoshop: **http://www.adobe.com/products/photoshop/ main.html**

Information about E-Commerce

The E-Commerce Guidebook: **http://www.online-commerce.com**
Web hosting reviews (searchable database): **http://www. webhostingratings.com**
Free comprehensive site comparing Web-hosting plans: **http://www. findmyhosting.com**
Free domain name search: **http://www.domainsearch.com**
Amazon.com: **http://www.amazon.com** (Click on "Marketplace" and "Join Advantage" from the home page.)
Barnes & Noble: **http://www.barnesandnoble.com** (Click on "Publisher and Author Guidelines" under "Services" from the home page.)

Information about Copyeditors and Printers

Editorial Freelancers Association: **http://the-efa.org** (See their directory of copyeditors, by state, at **http://66.241.221.102/ EFADirectory/select.asp**.)
Xlibris: **http://www2.xlibris.com/copyedit/index.asp**
BookMasters: **http://www.bookmasters.com/services/compcopyedit. htm**
How to interpret copyediting and proofreading marks: **http://www. neu.edu/styleguide/appendix_b.html**
Literary Market Place directory: **http://www.literarymarketplace. com** (For printers, click on "Manufacturing" under "Industry Services" in the sidebar menu.)
Book Printers for Small Publishers: **http://www.spawn.org/printers. htm**

Authoring Your Textbook or Instructional Material

Before you can publish your textbook or instructional material, you first must author it. While my focus in this book is on publishing rather than authoring, this chapter deals with some publishing-related authoring issues, considerations, and strategies, including the following.

- Establishing a daily schedule
- Deciding how and where to write
- Choosing computer hardware and software
- Drafting and editing text
- Securing illustrations

Authoring tasks are summarized in the figure.

Establishing a Daily Schedule

One of the secrets of finding enough time to complete a writing project is utilizing small chunks of time that occur in your schedule almost every day. Write for at least 30 minutes at about the same time daily. Many authors have used this strategy successfully. Even if you write only 30 minutes daily, you can complete a manuscript. As one author commented:

> The importance of a regular schedule—this same half hour every day—is vital; a definite rhythm is created both mentally and physically, and the writer automatically goes to his [or her] desk at that certain time, drawn by habit. The brain too...quickly learns to operate efficiently at such times.... Once the pattern of a daily half hour at a stated time is set, nothing short of disaster will keep you from writing.... The mere fact that such a routine is habit-forming...will condition you to greater output.

Famous Writers School, *Principles of Good Writing*, 1969, pp. 88, 91

I have used this strategy for the past 25 years. I write every morning (immediately after waking and having a cup or two of coffee) for 30 minutes to an hour. I've been able to draft manuscripts for 300- to 350-page books in approximately 18 months by doing so.

One doubt that you may have about this strategy is that you'd need time to think before you write, and consequently much (perhaps most) of each 30-minute period probably would be spent thinking. While only a half hour may be scheduled daily for writing, the preparation for writing is likely to take place, consciously or unconsciously, all day. Somerset Maugham, the novelist, commented in an interview that:

> The author does not only write while he's at his desk, he writes all day long, when he is thinking, when he is reading, when he is experiencing, everything he sees and feels is significant to his purpose and, consciously or unconsciously, he is forever storing and making over his impressions.

Famous Writers School, *Principles of Good Writing*, 1969, p. 91

Two authors whom I have interviewed made similar comments.

> I write almost every night. And I think about it during the day and get thoughts organized in my mind so that when I come home I can sit down and actually do it. I have done a whole chapter in one sitting because I had it all in my head.

> The book constantly is on my mind. How do I want to conceptualize this? Can I say it this way? In thinking about it, I found I was preoccupied by it almost 24 hours a day.

While my focus here has been on finding time for writing, the same strategy can be used to find time for publishing as well. That is, spending a half hour or so a day on publishing tasks can enable you to publish your textbooks or instructional materials and market them successfully.

Deciding How and Where to Write

You have several decisions to make before beginning to write. One concerns what medium you will use for writing. While almost all authors now use a computer with word-processing software, although some still use a typewriter or a legal pad. Before 1980 almost all books published during this century were drafted on a typewriter. While I now use a computer, my first four books were written with a 1950s vintage manual Royal typewriter. The novelist James Michener, incidentally, continued to draft his books on vintage manual typewriters well into the 1990s (Michener, 1992).

Almost all authors switched from typewriters to computers for several reasons. First, editing does not require retyping pages. Sentences and paragraphs can be added, deleted, modified, and relocated without having to retype pages. Second, editing is facilitated through utilities that check spelling and grammatical usage and suggest synonyms. Third, manuscripts for new editions are easier to prepare because retained material can be cut and pasted rather than retyped. And finally, it is possible to copyedit and typeset from word processor files.

Some authors still draft chapters initially on legal pads. In one informal survey of college textbook authors during the early 1990s, 27 percent acknowledged doing so. Several of the authors whom I interviewed commented that drafting chapters in this way improves the quality of their writing, because they are able to consider alternatives to every word, phrase, sentence, and paragraph while keyboarding what they wrote on paper. Furthermore, they reported, drafting chapters on paper enables them to work on their manuscript anywhere and for as long as they want. They are not restricted, for example, by the amount of power remaining in the battery of a laptop computer, although wireless satellite-powered laptops are removing even this obstacle.

A significant percentage of the material I wrote during the past 29 years I initially drafted on paper in pads or three-ring binders and sometimes sheets folded in a shirt pocket. Drafting material in this way both enabled me to work on a project wherever I was and caused me to devote more time to editing while keyboarding than I would have otherwise.

There are, of course, other ways to draft manuscripts. One author I interviewed uses a tape recorder, a legal pad, and a computer.

> The way I write is I think a great deal about what I'm going to write. And I'll be concentrating on a given subject area which will constitute a chapter eventually. And I keep thinking about that. And then I work up the illustrations— charts and graphs—and examples. Then, having done that preliminary work on the subject, I will dictate into a tape recorder the whole chapter at once around all of those examples and illustrations. I have a chapter. So, I play it back to myself and I write it down in longhand in pencil and I revise it as I write. Then I type the whole thing and I revise as I'm doing this. This is a real rough draft. Next, I retype it again in more finished copy. That's what the publisher gets. I have rewritten and retyped three times. That's exactly the way I write. I've done it all my life.

There is no one right way to write!

Another decision you will have to make is where to write. Some authors use their office, some a workspace at home, and some both. If you are using computers at both your home and office, the computers will have to be compatible or able to accept file sharing or file transfer. One strategy is to email documents back and forth to yourself as attachments as you work on them in different locations.

Some authors, including myself, occasionally write in hotel rooms and lobbies, airports, and restaurants. As an early morning person, when I travel, I usually write at a restaurant for several hours while having breakfast.

It is advantageous to be able to work on a manuscript wherever you are. Rather than relying solely on large blocks of time for drafting, you will be able to take advantage of the small blocks that occur almost daily. "Found time" of 30 minutes or less may occur at work between classes or meetings, while traveling, or at home when you wake up early or would otherwise be tempted to watch television when you really have no interest. Even only a few minutes may enable you to make significant progress on a project. For example,

> William Carlos Williams, the physician-poet…turned out a large body of work during office hours by writing *single lines of poetry between patients.* Williams kept pad and pencil in his desk drawer and between the time one patient left his office and the next entered, he would scribble a line—and sometimes two or more!

Famous Writers School, *Principles of Good Writing*, 1969, p. 90

Few authors can be productive if they are constantly interrupted. Creating an interruption-free environment in your home can be difficult, however, particularly if you have young children. An author I interviewed attempted to create time and space to write in a rather novel way.

> When my daughter was in fifth grade I did much of my writing at home, and she would sometimes come in and interrupt me. Once, to discourage her from doing it, I said, "Becky, every time you come in here and interrupt me it costs me ten cents a word." Well, she came in after that and said, "I've got a great idea, Dad. Put "THE END" at the end of every chapter and then you can make another twenty cents."

Choosing Computer Hardware and Software

At a minimum, you're going to need a computer and printer with appropriate word processing software. The computer can be either a PC or Mac with a disk drive for floppies or CDs (or both) and an inkjet or laser printer. Today many authors use CD writers to burn their final manuscripts onto CDs. If you are planning to create camera-ready copy, the faster and better quality your printer the better. Also, as mentioned in Chapter 5, a 600+ dpi printer will yield pages that are closer in appearance to professional typesetting. If your publication contains photographs or representational drawings, you will need a printer capable of at least 1200 dpi. Otherwise, you can arrange to have your pages printed at a service bureau or elsewhere.

Two other pieces of hardware that you may need are an external modem, if needed, and a scanner. You will need to be linked to the Internet by a dial-up telephone modem, cable TV, or DSL Ethernet. DSL or cable is preferred for speed. A scanner pulls drawings and photographs into your chapter documents, unless you use digitized images that you create yourself using a digital camera or download from the Internet. You also will need a scanner if you plan to import printed or typed text using OCR software.

Your word processing program may have adequate page-layout or desktop publishing capabilities. Alternatively, you may need a program such as PageMaker or Quark Xpress. Most commercial printers prefer to print books from Quark files generated on a Mac (or PDF files), and may convert whatever files you send to meet their needs. Larger printers especially usually will accept and convert PC files as needed. If your book is being professionally designed and typeset rather than photographed as is, then the format of your manuscript disk files will not matter.

Three other types of software you may need are communication software, OCR software, and graphics software. Communication programs, which typically are built into your computer, give you access to the Internet and capabilities such as sending and receiving virtual faxes. OCR software converts text in documents (e.g., books or articles) into digital files that you can then manipulate through word processing. As explained earlier, graphics software enables you to create and modify drawings and photographs.

Drafting and Editing Text

For any project, you may find it helpful to prepare an outline before beginning to write. Good outlines help authors develop their thoughts logically and ensure that they cover all relevant topics, but without repetition. Most authors revise their working outlines while writing. New topics and better orderings of topics often occur to them while they are drafting. Consequently, the content of an outline should be regarded as tentative and subject to change throughout the drafting and editing process. I have authored about 25 books, mostly textbooks, and in no instance was the final outline identical to the initial one. Utilities for outlining are a component of both Microsoft Word and Corel WordPerfect. Once you have developed a reasonably complete first approximation of your outline, you should begin to write. Headings, sentences, and paragraphs can be copied and cut from your outline and pasted into the manuscript to keep you on track without rekeyboarding.

An effective attitude toward writing is to view it as a two-stage process. The first stage is getting down what you want to communicate, and the second is revising (editing) what you have written so that your message will be clear to the reader. The following remarks by Roger H. Garrison indicate the importance of achieving clarity (Famous Writers School, *Principles of Good Writing*, 1969, p. 92):

> Nearly all first drafts, even those of skilled writers, are verbose, awkward, and disconnected. Ideas have gaps in one place and overflow in another. Sentences and paragraphs are turgid and muddy. A first draft is like the slow emerging of a statue from a block of stone. The rough shape of the work may be plain, but there is much chisel work and smoothing to be done.

During the first stage, you should not be too concerned about word choice, spelling, grammatical usage, or sentence structure. If ideas occur to you for improving these, do a little editing, so long as this does not interfere with getting down your thoughts. Most experienced authors do very little editing before they finish a first draft of a manuscript. However, if knowing you have many errors disturbs you and keeps you from moving forward, then do what editing you think is necessary to make you feel comfortable. During this first stage, you also may not wish to be too concerned about checking information for accuracy or currency.

Doing so can interfere with getting down your thoughts. It is important, however, to have a strategy for identifying the information that needs to be checked for accuracy. The writer James Michener recommends the following strategy (1992, p. 7):

> Because in this first draft I am struggling to outline a narrative progression, I do not interrupt my thought processes to check with almanacs, atlases, or encyclopedias to verify dates, spellings, or other data; I am aware as I type that I don't have the facts, but I am secure in the knowledge that I'll be able to find them when I go back to edit. So, for uncertainties I...type in what I guess to be the correct information adding immediately after the data a series of question marks: 'Magna Carta was granted by King John???? in 1215????,' with the intention of dealing with them later when I have my research books at hand. I advocate this strategy because the forward motion of the narrative is all-important.

You can use your word processor's global Search or Find command to quickly locate the information you must check for accuracy by asking it to find all instances of ????. (Actually, no more than two question marks would be necessary.) Make sure you eliminate all those question marks, including facts in source citations, before you send your manuscript out for peer review.

The most important part of the manuscript drafting process is communicating your unique knowledge. Your publication will be judged primarily on the usefulness of it's content to readers. While you certainly should strive to make your writing clear and interesting and your spelling and grammatical usage correct, your copyeditor can be expected to fill the gap.

If there are serious problems with your writing that you're unable to correct, you may be able to contract with someone to rewrite the manuscript, possibly a colleague or a professional freelance writer. The contract with such a person would state that for services rendered he or she will be paid an hourly fee, given a percentage of the royalty income, or designated as a co-author. See the chapter appendix for some sources of authoring assistance.

You should consistently follow the style set out by authorities in your field, such as the APA, MLA, CBA, Chicago, or other style. Otherwise, while your primary focus should be on eliminating grammatical and spelling errors and on communicating clearly to your intended audience, you should also focus on presenting material interestingly. The amount of attention that people will pay is determined in part by how interestingly you write. Any topic can be made interesting through good writing.

There are several strategies you can use to make your writing more interesting to a reader who otherwise lacks a high level of interest in your topics. One strategy is to include concrete examples that both clarify concepts and are relevant to the readers' interests. In a textbook on clinical research design intended for students majoring in speech pathology, for example, some of the examples used to illustrate single-subject research designs describe therapy outcomes.

Another strategy for interesting writing is to write in an "oral" style—one closer to a lecture style than in a typical journal article. One way to achieve this writing style is to dictate first drafts on a tape recorder or use your computer's voice recording utility. A second way to achieve oral rhythms is to read aloud what you have written, visualizing your intended audience.

Political correctness is another issue to consider when editing your manuscript. What you publish should be as free as possible of language that is sexist, racist, classist, ageist, or otherwise likely to be strongly offensive to readers. For example, avoid using the masculine pronouns (*he*, *his*) inappropriately to refer to professionals or subjects in a field of study. You can do this easily by pluralizing the subject of the sentence and using the plural pronouns (e.g., *they*).

Securing Illustrations

You may be able to acquire photographs and drawings from professional books, journal articles, advertisements, Web sites, and product catalogs. Some professional and scientific journals will allow you to use photographs and drawings from papers after paying a fee, if the authors of those papers are agreeable. Also, some academic and professional book publishers—particularly university presses—may allow you to use illustrations from books they have published either without cost or for a nominal fee. Furthermore, copies of photographs and drawings from advertisements and product catalogs often can be acquired and used without cost if their source is acknowledged.

Other sources of "free" photos are local and state historical societies and executive agencies such as NASA and the National Archives. You also will find archives of copyright-free images online. Note, however, that any photograph you use is never entirely cost free, because you will have to pay to have halftones made to reproduce them in your publication.

Today almost all textbook illustration is created from drawings and photographs that are scanned into a computer. If you are not the copyright owner, you will have to secure written permission to reproduce them. A scanned drawing or photograph can be manipulated or retouched in a number of ways. For example, its size can be increased or decreased. If it is in color, it can be converted to black and white. Its contrast can be increased or decreased. If it is a drawing, portions of it can be erased and new elements (e.g., labels) added. If it is a photograph, a part of the image (e.g., a distracting background) can be eliminated, or a part of another photograph (e.g., a more appropriate background) can be added to it. You can make many of these modifications yourself, even if you think you have little or no artistic ability.

Drawings

There are two options for creating graphs and other drawings that you are unable to acquire from other sources. You can have them created by a freelance illustrator from rough sketches or from data, or you can generate them yourself on your computer. While the first of these options might yield more attractive art, drawings that you create might more accurately communicate what you want to say. Doing your own graphics is also a lot cheaper.

Software is available for converting sets of numbers into graphs suitable for publication. Almost any type of graph can be drawn in this way. You supply the data and a description of the type of graph you want and the computer does the rest. You can use either a program intended exclusively for this purpose (e.g., Datagraph Professional) or one that includes this capability among others (e.g., Microsoft Excel, which also creates spreadsheets). You can submit graphs drawn in this way as disk files and as printouts. Most publishers prefer to have graphs and other drawings submitted on disk because they reproduce with higher quality and do not have to be scanned.

Programs also are available for making drawings other than

graphs, such as flow charts and organizational charts. Producing such a chart usually entails drawing or selecting geometric shapes (e.g., rectangles), arranging them appropriately on a page, connecting them with lines or arrows, and placing text in (or adjacent to) them. With a drawing program, every element (i.e., geometric shape, connecting line, word) is a separate object that can be moved or modified without affecting other elements. Consequently, you can correct mistakes easily.

Another alternative is to modify a version of an existing drawing by removing or adding elements or changing text. Be sure to credit the source. If the resulting drawing is recognizably similar to the original, you should request permission from the copyright hold to reproduce the modified drawing. An exception is if the drawing is generic, such as a representation of the DNA chain or a food pyramid, in which case permission to reproduce may not be necessary. Unfortunately, there are no generally accepted guidelines for what constitutes a generic drawing. Consequently, even though it may not be necessary to obtain permission to reproduce a drawing that most people would classify as generic, it probably would be a good idea not to take chances.

You probably will have to rely on a freelance illustrator for complex art, such as maps and anatomical or architectural drawings. Producing these kinds of illustrations can be quite expensive, so you should also consider getting permission to use existing drawings. Even if the fee for reproducing them is not nominal, the amount probably will be less than what you would have to pay to have them drawn. Copyright law and the permissioning process for text and illustrations are the subjects of Chapter 10.

Photographs

There are other ways to get the photographs you need that are not available for free or a nominal fee. You can take the photographs yourself, have them taken by a professional photographer, or purchase the use of them from an agency that rents stock photographs. If you have access to a camera—such as a 35mm single-lens reflex, large format, or digital camera—and the skill, you may be able to take at least a few of the photographs you need. You may also be able to capture stills from videotapes that you made with a camcorder. The quality, though not high, may be adequate for your purpose. Note that if people in your photographs can be recognized, you should be careful to have them sign a model release form (see the chapter appendix). Images showing registered trademarks also must be cleared for use, and you should have any foreign language writing in images translated to ensure its appropriateness for your purpose or book.

If you need photographs of a general nature (e.g., candid photographs of children) and are unable to take them yourself or find them as free sources, it may be cheaper to get them from a stock a stock photo agency. The larger stock photo agencies have hundreds of thousands of photographs in their files. Taken by professional photographers, the photos are not sold but are rented out for non-exclusive one-time use. Examples of stock agency sources are listed in the chapter appendix.

As mentioned previously, two other sources for photographs of from 1860 to the present are the Library of Congress and the National Archives. Both charge very little for them. An 8 x 10 black-and-white print from the National Archives cost less than $25.00 when this chapter was released for production. You will find more information about securing illustrations in Chapter 8.

Authoring References and Online Resources

Writing and Editing Aids

BOOKS:
Authoring Books and Materials for Students, Academics, and Professionals, by Franklin H. Silverman (Praeger, 1998).
The Elements of Style, 4th edition, by William Strunk, Jr. and E.B. White (Allyn and Bacon, 2000).
Handbook for Academic Authors, 4th edition, by Beth Luey (Cambridge University Press, 2002).
Writing and Developing Your College Textbook, by Mary Ellen Lepionka (Atlantic Path Publishing, 2003).
Handbook of Nonsexist Writing: For Writers, Editors, and Speakers, 2nd edition, by Casey Miller and Kate Swift (Harper & Row, 1988).

ORGANIZATIONS:
Text and Academic Authors Association (TAA): **http://www. TAAonline.net**
Society of Academic Authors (SA2**): http://sa2.info**
Educational Writers Association (EWA): **http://www.ewa.org**
The Authors Guild (AG): **http://www.authorsguild.org**

DATA AND SOFTWARE:
Monument Information Resource (MIR**): http://www.mirdata.com.**
See their searchable database of reviews of college textbooks for faculty members at **http://www.facultyonline.com/default.asp**
Links to all academic style manuals at Purdue's Online Writing Lab: **http://www.owl.english.purdue.edu/handouts/research/index** *(Click on "Resources for Documenting Sources" under "Research Skills and Resources.")*
Examples of outlining and online researching software: **http://www. casesoft.com/notemap/, http://www.academixsoft.com/, http:// www.powerresearcher.com/**

Working with Illustrations and Photographs

BOOKS:
James A Michener's Writer's Handbook, by James Michener (Random House, 1992).
2003 Photographer's Market, by Donna Poehner and Sara Spears, eds.

(Photographer's Market, 2003).

Getting It Printed: How to Work with Printers and Graphic Imaging,
3rd edition, by Mark Beach and Eric Kenly (North Light Books,
1999).

SOFTWARE:

Example of datagraph software: **http://www.kidasa.com/
upgradenow/eightvaluesets.html**

Microsoft Excel: **http://www.microsoft.com/office/excel/**

Adobe Illustrator: **http://www.adobe.com/products/illustrator/
main.html**

PHOTO SOURCES:

Library of Congress Prints and Photographs Online Catalog: **http://
www.loc.gov/rr/print/catalogabt.html**

National Archives (NARA Information about obtaining copies of
photographs or records): **http://www.archives.gov/research_
room/obtain_copies/reproductions_overview.html**

Leading stock photo agencies: **http://www.indexstock.com/default.
asp, http://creative.gettyimages.com/photodisc/, http://www.
comstock.com/web/default.asp, http://www.corbis.com**

FORMS AND MODELS:

Information and ideas on peer review: **http://carbon.cudenver.
edu/~mryder/peer/peer_review.html, http://www.exploit-lib.
org/issue5/peer-review/, http://www.firstmonday.dk/issues/
issue4_4/proberts/**

Sample model release forms: **http://www.dpcorner.com/all_about/
releases.shtml**

7

Print and Electronic Self-Publishing

One decision you will have to make is how to manufacture and distribute your textbook or instructional material. There are several options that a self-publisher can utilize, singly or in combination. While these options are assignable to one of two categories—electronic or print—there is overlap between them. The oldest and most popular options for publishing textbooks and instructional materials use printed sheets of paper that are folded, bound, and cut, or are otherwise packaged. Essential information about photo-offset printing and the other publishing options follows.

Photo-Offset Printing

Most books and materials are printed in the traditional photo-offset process. The printer photographs the camera-ready pages you provide and from the resulting negatives creates aluminum or polyester (Silvermaster) printing plates. While aluminum plates reproduce better detail better in high quality photographs and delicate line drawings than polyester plates, they are more expensive. A combination can be used—e.g., an aluminum plate for the cover of a book and polyester ones for the pages. The plates are then inked and printed on paper in an offset press.

If the publication is a book, four to 32 pages will be printed on a single sheet of paper. Each 32-page sheet—referred to as a full signature—is then folded to form a set of consecutively numbered pages. If 16 pages are printed on a sheet, the sheet is referred to as a 16-page signature, or half signature. A 160-page book would require five full signatures, while a 176-page book would require five full signatures plus a half signature. Thus, printers buy paper in signatures as the unit amount. The folded signatures are assembled, bound, and cut to trim size to produce a book. In figuring your book length, you should plan to use entire signatures and half signatures in even multiples (for example a seven-signature book—224 pages). You will have to pay the same for each full signature or half signature your book uses, whether or not all the pages contain printed matter.

Decisions you will have to make when printing by photo-offset affect both the appearance of a publication and its cost. These decisions include the following.

- Page size (trim size)
- Number of pages
- Paper and ink
- How illustrations are provided
- Type of binding
- Cover paper and printing
- Copy provided
- Number of copies

Page Size

Three standard page sizes for books are 5.5 x 8.5 inches, 6 x 9, and 8.5 x 11. The smaller page sizes are common for books other than textbooks, partly because illustrations would appear too small. The small column width makes text very readable, however, and this is suitable for either hard or soft cover binding and is the most economical to print.

The 6 x 9 trim size also is very readable and suitable for either hard or soft cover binding. It is probably the most common size for upper tier textbooks and professional books. The extra half an inch provides a little more space for illustrations. It tends, however, to cost a little more to print books in this larger size. The 8.5 x 11 page size often is suitable for textbooks that contain illustrations, tables, or workbook activities that have to be fairly large to communicate effectively. This size usually is the only alternative when a textbook or instructional material is going to be packaged in 3-ring binders.

Other page sizes are possible. For example, el-hi and undergraduate textbooks typically have an 8 x 10 or 7 x 10 trim size. However, because they require non-standard press setups, they tend to be more expensive to print than standard trim sizes.

Number of Pages

Page count includes front matter (title page, etc.), end matter (e.g., index), and text. Because your book will be printed in signatures, you will want to try to limit the number of pages to the space available in the book's last signature. The more signatures there are in a book, the more expensive it will be to print it!

Publishers determine page count in advance so they can purchase the correct number of signatures for a print run in advance at favorable terms. Authors then must meet this page count, cutting text if the book goes over length. As a self-publisher, you, too, will need to determine length in advance and manage length outcomes.

Paper and Ink

Unless you are publishing an art book with high-quality four-color reproductions, most printers will recommend a 50- or 60-pound white, uncoated, offset paper. The higher the weight is, the thicker the book and the heavier and more opaque the paper. Because the paper is heavier, the book will be bulkier and the more it will cost to store and ship the books.

The thickness, or bulk, of book paper is measured in ppi (pages per inch). The heavier the paper is, the lower the ppi (i.e., the fewer pages there are in an inch). Consequently, to calculate the width of a book's spine, you need to know both the number of pages in the book and the ppi of the paper on which it will be printed. You need this information to design a wraparound hard or soft cover for it.

While you may want archival acid-free paper for an art book, most textbooks use standard paper. This grade of paper is the least expensive and contains acid, which causes the paper to deteriorate eventually. If the information in your book will only be useful for years, rather then decades, and if you plan to revise it every few years, then this deterioration is unlikely to be a cause for concern. Acid-free paper tends to be more expensive than standard paper and perhaps should be reserved for art or scholarly books with information likely to be of value for decades but unlikely to be revised.

If you are environmentally conscious, you may want to consider using recycled paper. It is a little more expensive than standard book paper but can be acid-free. If you do use recycled paper, you may want to print the recycling symbol and the following statement on the copyright page of your book: "This book is printed on recycled paper."

Almost all educational books are printed on white paper. Off-whites (e.g., creams) and other colors are available but tend to be a little more expensive than white. Other types of papers (such as coated papers or vellums) may be used for books that contain high-quality drawings or photographs. If you wish to use a special type of paper, find a book containing it to show to your printer as a sample.

The pages in almost all textbooks are printed in black ink. A second color (spot color) sometimes is used to emphasize or categorize material or to aid in illustration. The use of a second color increases printing costs, however, because signatures have to be passed through the press twice. Four-color printing, as described in Chapter 4, is more involved and expensive.

Illustrations Provided

You can submit illustrations—both drawings and photographs—either "as is" or in digital form as computer files. It requires less time to prepare them for printing if they are submitted in digital form. Consequently, your costs will be lower if you provide illustrations on disk.

If drawings are created with a computer, submitting digital files to the printer should create no problem. Files that exceed the capacity of a diskette (1.44 MB) can either be compressed or recorded on high capacity disks (e.g., burned onto CDs) or transmitted to the hard drive of the printer's server via email, fax modem, or FTP file transfer. Files you can transfer include scans of art. That is, you can scan drawings and photos that were not created digitally into your computer. If you do not have a high-quality scanner, however, you should submit the originals on paper for the printer to scan or photograph.

Kind of Binding

After the signatures are folded and cut into pages, the pages are bound together. Six binding methods used for textbooks include perfect binding, case binding (hard cover), comb or spiral binding (plastic or wire), 3-ring (loose-leaf) binding, and saddle stapling. Each method is described below.

Perfect Binding is the method currently used most frequently for textbooks. After the pages of a book are collated, folded, and trimmed, the spine edge is ground off, leaving a rough surface. Hot flexible glue then is applied to the spine, and a wraparound cover is attached. The minimum number of pages required for a perfect bound book is approximately 40 (20 sheets of paper). However, usually it is not possible to print the title and author's name on the spine of the book if it contains fewer than 80 pages.

Case (or Hard Cover) Binding is the most durable and expensive of the book binding methods. The difference in cost between case and prefect binding often is approximately a dollar a copy. The surface of the cover usually is cloth with the title and author's name printed on the front. If a case bound book contains at least 100 pages, the title and author's name are printed on the spine also. In one method of case binding, the book is perfect bound and glued into a hard cover. In another method, the page signatures are sewn together, reinforced, and then attached to the hard cover. Sewn books tend to be more durable than glued books but are significantly more expensive.

Spiral or Comb Binding is ideal for books that must lie flat when opened, such as workbooks or manuals. Plastic combs and wire spirals can, of course, be used for almost any kind of book. Although almost any number of pages can be spiral or comb bound, it usually is not recommended for books having fewer than 48 pages (24 sheets of paper). The cover of a book with this binding can be thin or heavy cardboard. While both the front and back covers can be printed like those for a perfect bound book, the title and author's name will not appear on the spine unless they are printed on the plastic comb, which tends to be expensive. Since books are usually displayed on shelves at libraries and bookstores with only their spines visible, the lack of a title and author name on a book's spine may reduce sales. In addition, libraries typically do not purchase spiral or comb bound books. Wire spiral binding can be used instead of plastic comb binding for books that must lie flat when opened. While the title and author usually do not appear on the spines of books that are bound this way, it is possible to have a wire spiral binding with a wraparound cover and a printed spine.

Three-Ring (Loose-Leaf) Binding is another method you can use for books that must lie flat when opened. It is the only binding method that allows a user to keep material up-to-date by replacing, removing, and adding pages. The page size is almost always 8.5 x 11 and three-hole punched. The front and back covers as well as the spine can be printed directly on a binder or on sheets of paper that are inserted behind clear plastic coverings on the front, back, and spine of a binder. Printed tabbed separators can be added to facilitate locating chapters or sections quickly.

In Saddle Stapling, a book is stapled directly through its centerfold—hence the term "saddle." Two or three staples are used, and it is most practical for books that are no more than a quarter-inch thick (about 80 pages of 60-pound paper). Pages for 5.5 x 8.5 stapled books are printed on 8.5 x 11 sheets, and those for 8.5 x 11 books are printed on 11 x 17 inch sheets. Covers can be printed on the front and back, but not on the spine. The right sides of books that are bound in this way can be trimmed so that inner sheets do not protrude further than outer ones when the block of pages is folded and stapled.

Cover Paper and Printing

The standard cover paper for perfect, comb, spiral, and saddle-stapled bindings is a 10- or 12-point C1S (coated one side) cover stock. Covers usually are coated to protect them and enhance the color. Several kinds of coating are available. Ask the printers from whom you request estimates what types of cover papers they use and the advantages of each. Also ask for samples. If a book is going to be case (hard) bound, request samples of the fabrics that printers have available. Also request illustrations and prices if your book is going into a 3-ring binder.

For perfect bound, spiral or comb bound, and stapled books, printing in one color costs the least. Printing a cover in one color doesn't necessarily result in all of the text and graphics on it being the same shade ("darkness"). By a process known as screening, one-color printing can produce the full gray scale in addition to black, so that some elements (i.e., text and graphics) can be made to appear lighter or darker than others. And by using white cover paper and having some of the text drop-out white, you can make a single color cover appear varied in color. As explained previously, for high quality full color text and graphics, a cover has to be run through the press four times—once for each of the three primary colors and once for black.

For some case bound books, the covering of the front and back cover boards is paper and is printed the same way as for books bound by other methods. Other case bound books have cloth-covered boards. The title and authors name(s) are stamped (often with a metallic foil) on the spine and possibly also the front cover. If a case bound book has a dust jacket, the jacket is printed by the same process as is used for the covers of perfect bound, plastic or wire spiral or comb bound, and saddle stapled books. For 3-ring binding, the cover is printed either directly on the binder or on sheets of paper that are slipped under the transparent plastic coverings on its front and back covers and spine. Printing also can be done directly on the binder, usually by a process of silk screening.

Copy Provided

Pages can be submitted in camera-ready printed form or on computer disk. Submitting pages in camera-ready form is the less expensive option, while having pages designed and laid out by a computer artist to print from disk is the most expensive option. You can decrease this cost significantly by using your word processor's program for identifying and defining a formatted style for each type of element in your manuscript. For example, you can highlight a regular paragraph of text and define or format it as the template for every paragraph of that type. Likewise, you can define a style for each level of heading you use, each type of listed (bulleted, numbered, etc.), excerpts, examples, figure titles, captions, etc., until all elements of your manuscript have been defined.

These styles become saved as part of your document when you save it, and later, when your book is going into type from disk, the printing program will automatically design your pages. The resulting initial page proof greatly reduces the amount of time and effort that your printer's artist or layout person needs to spend to finalize your pages. Once you approve the design, your content is simply "poured" into it, and after you approve the corrected page proof, your book is printed from disk.

Number of Copies

The number of copies printed determines the cost per copy. The smaller the print run is, the higher the cost per copy. The cost per copy for printing 250 may be approximately half that for printing 100, and the cost per copy for printing 500 copies may be a third of that for printing 100. After 500, the savings are not as dramatic. The cost per copy for printing 3,000, for example, will be a little more than half that for printing 500. Having a printing of 3,000 copies would make sense economically if you expect to sell close to 3,000 copies in a year or so, but it would not make sense economically if you did not expect to sell this many. For this reason, many self-publishers have relatively small first printing (i.e., 500 to 1,000 copies). Doing so minimizes your investment up front and makes it unnecessary to store a large number of books. It also gives you an opportunity to correct errors before a second printing if, of course, sales justify further production. For textbooks and instructional materials, however, you should print more than you would expect to sell, because you will need to provide examination copies for potential course adopters and for reviewers.

Photocopies and Printouts

Printing also can be done on a photocopy machine. Both 5.5 x 8.5 and 8.5 x 11 pages can be printed out on either 8.5 x 11 or 11 x 17 sheets respectively. You can use standard weight book paper. Photocopied books can be bound by any of the methods described in the section on photo-offset printing, including case binding. Print on demand books usually are done this way.

This method of printing is most acceptable for books that contain only text and simple figures and tables. Photographs and drawings can be included, but the quality of reproduction is likely to be poorer than with photo-offset printing. However, it may be good enough for your purposes. Reproduction quality is likely to be better if you copy halftones of photographs or drawings rather than originals. Most local photocopy shops can produce such halftones.

There are several advantages to printing books in this way, because there is no minimum number you have to print. A single copy can be printed and bound. You can, therefore, reduce your initial investment by printing on demand (i.e., printing books after they are ordered). Another advantage is that you do not have to warehouse books. And you can correct errors that are brought to your attention before printing the books to fill your next order. The main disadvantage is that it tends to be much more expensive to print books in this way than by photo-offset. You can, of course, begin by photocopying a book and then switching to photo-offset if the book sells well enough to justify the expense. For textbooks, in which sales involve class sets for course enrollments one to four times a year, photocopying probably is not your best option.

It is best not to try to print out your textbook or instructional materials on your home computer printer for more than a few copies, however. Although both 5.5 x 8.5 and 8.5 x 11 pages can be printed out and bound using the spiral/comb or 3-ring notebook binding, printing in any quantity would be more expensive than photo-offset, more time consuming, and possibly damaging to your equipment, which is not designed for this use.

Short Runs, Long Runs, and Print on Demand

POD (Print On Demand) is worth considering as a viable option when your goal is to print paperback textbooks or instructional materials in short runs, even in batches as small as one copy. The quality of the book is comparable to that of books printed in other ways. This is not particularly surprising, since the machine on which they are printed can cost as much as a million dollars. The paperbacks they yield have four-color covers and perfect bindings, and even can have illustrations inside. The quality of the paper and printing is similar to that produced by other methods. POD books can even be case bound.

POD has both advantages and disadvantages for producing textbooks. Advantages include the following:

- You do not have to pay for having books printed before they are sold.
- You do not have to store books in your home or warehouse them before they are sold.
- You can keep books in print indefinitely.

Perhaps the main disadvantage is that the per-unit cost of POD books is higher than for traditional printing, and the cost remains constant even when print runs increase in size. Not investing a lot of money in printing up front and not having to warehouse many books at home may outweigh this disadvantage. Moreover, the higher per-unit cost difference between POD and traditional printing may be offset by the cost of having more books printed than can be sold. Having more books printed than can be sold reduces, at least a little, the difference in the per-unit cost between POD and traditional printing. Another disadvantage of POD is that printers specializing in it tend to be seen as vanity presses.

PQN (Print Quantity Needed) printing for per-unit cost falls between traditional offset printing and POD. It is cost effective for short runs—quantities from 100 to 2,000 copies. PQN produces 8 to 12 books at a time from a PDF file. There are no films or plates used as there are in traditional offset printing. PQN uses an electrostatic process (like a photocopy machine) that can even reproduce photographs and other graphics well. Unlike POD, per-unit costs drop as quantities increase. The quality of the paperbacks and case bound books produced by this process tend to be as high as those produced by POD and traditional offset printing. See the chapter appendix for examples of PQN and POD printers.

The offset printing process is traditional for long runs—2,000 or more copies. Unlike PQN or POD, a film or plate has to be prepared for printing each page, which adds to the cost. The per-unit cost of running fewer than 2,000 copies by offset tends to be higher than if the same number were produced on a PQN or POD basis. However, for runs of 2,000 or more copies by offset, the per-unit cost is lower. Almost any textbook or instructional material that can be printed by PQN or POD also can be printed by photo-offset.

Which Print Process Should You Use?

To review, the three most frequently used processes for printing a textbook are POD, PQN, and traditional photo-offset printing. POD might be most appropriate for small batches of textbooks, such as those ordered for particular courses at particular institutions. PQN probably would be most appropriate for batches of between 500 and 2,000 copies that you hope to sell. And traditional offset printing probably would be most appropriate for batches over 2,000 copies. There could be exceptions to this pattern, however. For example, it may be more economical to print textbooks for a large multi-section introductory course by PQN rather than POD.

Your strategy might be to start small and grow. The first edition of a textbook would have uncertain sales. Consequently, you might print a small number of between 500 and 1,500 copies using PQN. If copies sold well, you could print future batches using offset printing. Then, after many years or when adoptions fall off, you could use POD to satisfy the smaller demand—or you could revise and re-launch your textbook all over again.

Electronic Options

Until fairly recently, the only viable option for self-publishing books and materials was to do so on paper. This is no longer the case. There are now electronic options that store text and illustrations, not on paper, but as digital or magnetic images on a medium from which they can be translated by an electronic device into a form we are able to see and/or hear. Publishing a book electronically does not preclude also doing so in print. Just as books can be published in both hardcover and paperback editions, they can be published in both print and electronic editions.

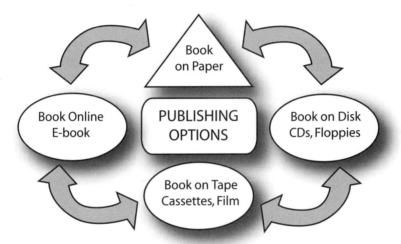

Digital Books

In electronic publishing you save the book on a 3.5-inch (1.44 MB) diskette or burn it onto a CD-ROM disk. The files for a 300-page book containing graphics can be stored on a diskette in compressed form. Compression software, such as Zip Disk, makes it possible to store larger files. For books with many pages and illustrations that have to be compatible with both PCs and Macs, a CD is best.

Digital books can be read on a computer monitor and may be printed in whole or part by a user. If the files are compressed, users transfer them to a hard drive and decompress the files to read them. A book published on disk can be encrypted and password-protected to discourage illegal copying. Each purchaser is given a unique password. When the purchaser enters the password the first time he or she reads the disk, the protection software binds the disk to the computer that he or she is using. The files cannot be read on another computer without a new password. Encryption and password protection also is intended to discourage hackers from illegally uploading some or all of the files to the Internet.

If you publish a digital book on diskettes, you can create disk copies from your hard drive as they are ordered, or you can have the copying done by a company that specializes in this process. Such a company also may encrypt and password-protect disks (though, of course, you can do both yourself if you purchase the necessary software). You also can print the labels for the disks yourself or have them printed by a firm that does so.

If you publish a digital book on CD-ROM, you can store the pages on your hard drive after laying them out and then burn the files onto a CD or have this done by a suitable firm. CD writers are becoming standard equipment on computers now, so that users can create as well as play CDs. If you have a CD writer, you can burn and distribute your own disks as copies are ordered, or you can have your master disk duplicated by a specialty house. You can use this process also for self-publishing instructional multimedia on CDs. CD contents can include audio and video segments as well as photographs, drawings, and text. Books and materials on disk have the same copyright protections as printed ones, although to date the laws have been more difficult to enforce for electronic media.

Publishing textbooks on disk can be advantageous in several ways. First, the cost of copying and distributing books on disk is relatively low. Both 3.5-inch disks and recordable CDs can be purchased for less than 50 cents each. This amount is considerably less than half the cost of having a book printed and bound by any method. Furthermore, it almost always costs less to package and ship books on disk than books printed on paper.

A second advantage of publishing textbooks in digital rather than print form is that errors can be corrected more easily, and they can be updated (revised) more readily. This is particularly true if books are printed on demand. A third advantage of publishing textbooks in digital rather than print form is that they can be made available to readers at a lower cost. Savings in production costs can be passed on to readers.

Disadvantages of publishing textbooks on disk are that the market may not want books in this form. Furthermore, your colleagues and potential adopters may not regard self-published digital books as "real." The method of printing and binding or otherwise manufacturing your textbook or instructional material should be based on your market research, if you expect to sell many copies.

Online Ebooks

Your electronic book can be published online rather than on disk. Users acquire your book by paying for and downloading files from the Internet rather than by purchasing a disk. The files may be downloaded to a PC or Mac or to a portable microcomputer-based device (such as Palm Pilot) intended for storing and reading electronic books (ebooks). Web sites from which ebooks are downloaded may be owned by their authors or by firms that offer self-publishers Internet marketing and order fulfillment services. These firms may additionally offer your book in printed, perfect-bound form, utilizing a POD printing and binding system.

Publishing a book electronically on the Internet eliminates (or has the potential to eliminate) "printing, binding, understocks, overstocks, freight, returns, shrinkage, warehouse space, damaged books, used books, the resale of review and 'comp' copies, violation of copyright, and deforestation" (Poynter, 1996, p. 389). Furthermore, publishing in this way makes an unlimited number of copies available for immediate purchase almost anywhere in the world, 24 hours a day, 365 days a year. And because the cost of electronic publishing is lower than print publishing, at least some of the savings can be passed on to the consumer.

Electronic publishing, incidentally, can be used to keep in print a book that a college textbook, professional book, or scholarly book publisher has declared "out of print." The pages of the book are scanned and the resulting file is posted on the Internet. The author is paid a royalty on each copy sold. Of course, you can post the file instead on your own Web site or on a noncommercial site to which you have access (e.g., one maintained by your institution or a professional association to which you belong). However, before you can legally self-publish your previously published book in this way, it is necessary to have the publisher revert the copyright to you.

Online publishing also can be used to revise a textbook, scholarly book, or professional book for which its original publisher is unwilling to authorize a new edition. If the publisher returns copyright to you, you can self-publish a revised edition in either electronic or print form. You can distribute the print form yourself or contract with an Internet firm that distributes books in print as well as electronic books.

An ebook, like a digital book on disk, can be encrypted and password-protected to discourage illegal copying. Books also can be uploaded as read-only PDF files, actual photographs of your finished pages. One advantage of publishing via the Internet is that the files can be read on both a PC and a Mac, whereas disks for PC and Mac usually must be produced separately.

PDF (Portable Document Format) is a universal file format that enables the display of book pages (or other documents) in readable form on the monitor of any computer or on the screen of some other appropriate device. PDF files can be stored on a disk, disk drive, or Web site and can be read on a screen or on paper, using Acrobat Reader or MS Reader or similar software. PDF preserves the fonts, images, graphics, and layouts on book pages. PDF files for a book are photographs of the pages. Your computer undoubtedly contains a program, such as Adobe Acrobat (see www.adobe.com), or a special utility for converting your word processing files to PDF, just as your computer probably has a way to convert your word processing files to HTML for Web site applications.

The PDF format is especially useful for publishing ancillaries to a textbook on disk. Because of universal portability, distributing ancillaries in PDF on disk tends to be inexpensive. Another way to distribute ancillaries in PDF format is to make them available on your company's Web site. The material could be read online and may or may not be made downloadable to the user's printer. Distributing ancillaries online is even less expensive than distributing CDs.

Audiobooks

Publishing an audiotape involves publishing audio tracks on diskettes or CDs, which are becoming increasingly popular. Many fiction and nonfiction best sellers are now published in both print and audiobook forms, and many scholarly and professional associations publish convention presentations on audiocassettes or disks. Textbooks and instructional materials that do not require illustrations also can be published in these ways.

One reason for the increased popularity of this form of publication is that most cars now have audiocassette and CD players built-in, and playing audiotapes or audiobooks while commuting or traveling is an advantageous use of time. Listening to lectures, for example, may be a practical way for students to acquire course information. Other materials suitable for self-publishing on audio are talks at invited lectures and workshops, papers or chapters that originally were published in printed form, and original new material.

Most scholars present information pertaining to their research and expertise in invited lectures or workshops, including presentations at conventions and conferences. If you record your presentations of this type yourself, or arrange to have them recorded, you can self-publish them on audiocassette or CD. Doing so can make the information available to persons who were unable to attend, and the content may be attractive to instructors as course supplements.

Just as fiction and nonfiction books for the general public are published in audiobook as well as in print form, textbooks can be also—either in their entirety or in abridged form. Using audio course materials could enable students to study while driving or could supplement distance learning programs.

You can script material for your audio and record it yourself of have others, such as professional speakers, present the material. Certainly you will need professional-quality recording equipment and a sound studio for any audio product that you expect to sell. Audiobooks can be particularly appropriate for textbooks in subjects involving auditory learning, such as speech, language, foreign languages, literature, and communication.

You can make copies of your audiotape or CD yourself on demand or arrange to have it duplicated by a firm that does this. You can print the labels for the cassette and box with your computer or arrange to have them printed. If your publication contains more than one cassette or CD, you can package it in an album. Audiobooks, like print books and ebooks, are protected by copyright law.

Videotape and Digitized Video

Videos, especially digital videos, are used as publishing media, particularly for instructional materials. Video on CD is more popular now than videotape for publishing instructional materials, mainly because it is less expensive to produce and can be distributed online and on disk, and thus is more flexible than magnetic tape or film for creating and displaying visual information.

Many scholars and educators, such as you, share their research and expertise at invited lectures and workshops. You could have your presentations recorded on videotape or digital video camera and self-publish them. Your tapes or disks could then be sold to colleges via instructors' adoptions for teaching purposes. Your video production also can consist of original or permissioned material that you script or collect to self-publish in this medium. Video can be a particularly useful medium for teaching students how to do something (e.g., how to perform a task, use instrumentation, or recognize diagnostic features).

You may hesitate to take on a videotape or digital video publication project because you lack some expertise in the technical aspects of video production or some necessary professional equipment. While it certainly would be nice if your publications were of professional quality, it may not be essential for your purposes. It is only essential that they be of sufficiently high quality to communicate what you intend to communicate. However, professional or commercial quality production is recommended if you are planning to sell your video.

As you can see, it is within your capability to undertake many, if not all, of the tasks associated with self-publishing, whether you are publishing on paper, on disk, on tape, online, or a combination. The more you can do, the more control you can have over your products and the more you can save on publishing costs. The next chapter offers advice on desktop publishing, in which you do just about everything!

Online Resources for Print and Electronic Publishing

Photo-Offset Printing

Net Read: Photo Offset: printing and binding: http://www.netread.com/howto/printers/

Glossaries of printing terms and concepts offered by commercial printers: http://www.gregathcompany.com/gloss.html, http://www.theprintguide.com/, http://www.mydesignprimer.com/printing/50020.html, http://www.dvdreplication.com/photoqualitycddvdprinting.html

University of Minnesota's Style Manual (with many terms relating to book production and manufacturing): http://www1.umn.edu/urelate/style/central%20index%20pages/p.html

Illustration of trim sizes: http://www.rjcom.com/cantmiss.asp

Information about book covers on commercial sites: http://www.bookcoverexpress.com, http://www.pneumabooks.com/covdesign.htm

Introduction to desktop publishing: http://desktoppub.about.com/cs/selfpublishing/

Information about ftp: http://www.ftpplanet.com, http://searchnetworking.techtarget.com/sDefinition/0,,sid7_gci213976,00.html

Printing on Demand and Print Quantity Needed

Lightning Source: http://www.lightningsource.com

iUniverse: http://www.iuniverse.com

Xlibris: http://www2.xlibris.com

Infinity: http://www.infinitypublishing.com

Article by Dan Poynter on PQN Printing: http://www.pma-online.org/scripts/shownews.cfm?id=352

Poynter's and Snow's U-Publish: http://www.u-publish.com/chap5.htm

Warnings and Cautions about Print on Demand: http://www.sfwa.org/beware/printondemand.html

Writer as Publisher information on print options: http://www.writeraspublisher.com/printing.html

Electronic Publishing

Information about e-books: http://www.knowledge-download.com

Desktop ebook publishing: http://www.desktopauthor.com

Electronic self-publishing: http://www.nwu.org/links/lnkepub.htm, http://escholarship.cdlib.org/books.html

Cautions about Print on Demand: http://www.sfwa.org/beware/printondemand.html

Links to collections of digital books: http://onlinebooks.library.upenn.edu

Yahoo's directory on compression: http://dir.yahoo.com/Computers_and_Internet/software/system_utilities/compression

How to passcode-protect content on your Web site: http://www.password-protection.com

Audio and Video Production

Creating Audiobooks from ebooks: http://www.portablevoice.com/ebooks.html

Information about recording media: http://www.totalmedia.com/catalog/catalog_home.asp?bustype=#

Examples of video production services: http://www.coliday.com/video/services.htm, http://videoservices.unl.edu/multimediasupport.cfm

Links for film and video production resources: http://www.people.memphis.edu/~commres/film_and_videotape_production_re.htm

Digital Media

Information on CD-ROM and other digital storage: http://www.cdrom-guide.com

Creating digital media for Palm ebook readers: http://www.palmdigitalmedia.com/

Digital Media Net for content providers: http://www.digitalmedianet.com

Example of digital media production services: http://www.lib.virginia.edu/clemons/RMC/dml.html

Preparing Pages for Print and Electronic Publication

Textbooks and instructional materials that contain words, drawings, or photographs and are intended for print, disk, or online publication all consist of paged manuscripts. The focus in this chapter is on preparing those pages. Specifically, what are some of the more important considerations for creating well-designed camera-ready print and electronic pages? These considerations include the following.

- Choice of fonts
- Keyboarding for typesetting
- Page design
- Preparing illustrations
- Printing pages for paper and electronic publication

Choice of Fonts

Hundreds of fonts are compatible with word processing and page layout programs. Most useful for textbooks and instructional materials are three font categories: serif, sans serif, and script. Serifs are short lines at the ends of the unconnected strokes of certain letters. For example, in the word *short*, serifs appear at the top and bottom of the "*h*" and at the bottom of the "*r*" and "*t*." Serifs differ slightly in appearance, depending on the typeface. A typeface in traditional printing is the surface of the etched or engraved metal that, when inked, makes an impression on paper (i.e., prints). A font is a complete set of type of the same typeface. For example, **boldface**, *italic*, Roman, ***bold italic,*** and SMALL CAPS are examples of fonts, also referred to as "styles." The serif typeface used in this book, called Caslon, has these fonts, among others.

Perhaps the most important fact about serif fonts is that they usually are easier to read than sans serif (without serifs) and script fonts (facsimiles of handwriting). They guide the movement of the eyes across a line of type. Consequently, serif fonts are almost always used for text in paragraphs, as in this book. San serif fonts lack short connecting lines at the ends of the unconnected strokes of letters. For example, *short* lacks serifs at the top and bottom of the "h" or other letters. Because text typeset in sans serif is more difficult to read than serif, they usually are reserved for special uses, such as headings, subheadings, and labels. Script fonts appear to have been handwritten or lettered with a calligraphy pen or brush. For example, *short* is in a script font. Script fonts may be used in cover designs and art but rarely are used on the pages of textbooks or instructional materials, unless facsimiles of handwriting are needed.

Fonts also are categorized in terms of size and proportionality. Character size is specified in points—a point is 1/72 of an inch. The point sizes used most often for typesetting paragraphs in textbooks are 9-point, 10-point, 11-point, and 12-point type. The space on which a line of type appears also is specified in points, so that a "10 on 12" type specification indicates 10-point type on a 12-point line. This book has 11 on 13 type. The space above and below a line of type is called "leading" (from the days when lead bars were used to separate rows of type). Leading can be increased or decreased to affect the appearance of type on a page or the number of lines per page.

Proportionality describes the width of the space occupied by a character, which is determined by the width of a character. For example, more space is allowed for "w" than for "i." If characters were all given equal space rather than proportional space, you would find it difficult to read a line of type. This book, like most books, is set in proportional type, because proportional type is easier to read and allows more text to fit on a page. About the only circumstances in which nonproportional typesetting is used are in art treatments or simulations of typewritten text.

Keyboarding for Typesetting

If you are designing your own textbook or instructional material and want it to appear to have been typeset professionally, you will have to observe certain conventions, expressed, for example, in Robin Williams' books, such as *The Mac Is Not a Typewriter* (2003). Some of the more important conventions are the following.

- Use proportional type unless you want material to appear to have been done on a typewriter.
- Use a serif font for regular text in paragraphs.
- Use only one space after periods, question marks, and other punctuation that separates two sentences.
- Check that opening and closing single and double quotation marks and apostrophes are "real" (i.e., the kind that curve).
- Do not use double hyphens for em-dashes, but use the character key that exists for this purpose. (Some word processing programs will automatically convert double hyphens to em-dashes, saving you the trouble.) Use em-dashes appropriately, only as a substitute for parentheses.
- Take advantage of the special characters in fonts— such as ¢, •, and ©—but use them consistently and only where appropriate (e.g., it is more appropriate to write out words like *cents* when they are embedded in sentences).
- Keyboard subscript and superscript characters appropriately.
- Use appropriate accent marks for foreign names and words. Almost all fonts intended for typesetting paragraphs contain them.
- Do not underline words that should be italicized but italicize them.
- Rarely (if ever) use words typeset all in caps or underlined words or phrases for emphasis within paragraphs. Blocks of text set all in caps or underlined are more difficult to read and may alter the spacing of lines. If necessary, italicize or boldface words instead to emphasize them, but use these devices appropriately and consistently (e.g., to highlight vocabulary items in instruction).
- Do not use the space bar to line up words and

numbers. Use tabs instead.

- Use a tab, rather than the space bar, for first-line paragraph indents. Doing so is faster and provides a more uniform indent for proportional fonts. Ideally, you should define a style for first-line paragraphs in your document formatting.
- Use the hanging paragraph command, rather than the space bar, to line up hanging paragraphs (like this one).
- As a general rule of thumb, use hard returns only at the end of headings and paragraphs.

Avoid "widows and orphans" whenever possible by copy fitting—adding, substituting, or deleting words or characters to make copy fit into the width of a line or the depth of a page. A "widow" is a paragraph in which the last line contains fewer than seven characters, and an "orphan" is a paragraph's last line when it runs over to the top of the next column or page. The next section describes some typesetting conventions pertinent to page design.

Page Design

An effective page design neither calls attention to itself nor detracts from the information you intend to present. Rather, the design facilitates communication. How information is laid out on the pages of a textbook determines how well the book communicates to students and how professional it looks to adopters. Textbook pages that contain long paragraphs of small type and little white space, for example, are less likely to hold a student's attention (and hence communicate less well) than pages with briefer paragraphs, easily readable type, and adequate white space.

The four major decisions that have to be made when designing the pages for a textbook include (Miles, 1987):

- page size;
- grid—i.e., the layout for the items on the pages;
- typography (i.e., fonts) used;
- and white space used.

These are four major decisions that have to be made about the graphic page design for a textbook. A number of how-to books provide this information. One that I found particularly helpful was Miles (1987).

An amateurish book design really stands out. Perhaps the most common error that self-publishers make is putting too much on each page. They tend to use too many different typefaces, fonts, and styles on a page. They also tend to use too many different page grids. The goal is to use the minimum number of fonts and grids on a page necessary to hold students' attention and communicate content effectively. Students should not be aware of page design, only the information presented!

Page layouts can significantly influence the likelihood that textbooks and instructional materials will communicate what your intend. To begin to develop an intuitive understanding of what constitutes effective page designs, examine a number of textbooks or instructional materials that are similar in structure and content to what you intend to self-publish. While doing so consider the following questions:

- What elements do those pages contain and how are the elements arranged on the page?
- Are some pages laid out in ways that make them more appealing to read? If so, in what ways do those page layouts differ from less appealing designs?

In evaluating page designs consider the following elements.

- Fonts used—the number, size, and type (e.g., serif, sans serif, script)
- Amount and arrangement of white space (i.e., blank space free of text and illustrations)
- Length of lines of text and amount of spacing between lines
- Use of headings and subheadings
- Type style(s) of words, headings, and phrases that are set off from text or emphasized in some way
- Use of color or gray scale to make material stand out.
- Use of line justification and word hyphenation
- The use of headings and subheadings

There can be other decisions that affect the appeal of page layouts, discussed in the following sections. See the chapter appendix for leads to more information.

Margins

The first decision you have to make when designing a single-column page layout for a textbook or instructional material is the measurements for the head, foot, inside, and outside margins. The two side margins are designated as inside and outside rather than left and right because on facing pages they are reversed (i.e., the inside margin in an open book is on the right side of the left page and left side of the right page). Thus, the inside margin is always the side nearest the spine of the book. Here are usual margins for a 5.5 x 8.5 book page.

> Head: 3/4 inch
> Foot: 7/8 inch
> Inside: 1/2 inch
> Outside: 5/8 inch

Note that the head margin is narrower than the foot margin. If the head margin is the same width as the foot margin or wider, the text will look as if it is falling off the page. The assumption here is that binding will consume approximately 3/16 of an inch of the inside margin of each page, thereby making the two inside margins as seen together approximately the same width as each outside margin.

Commercial textbook publishers often increase outside margin width to an inch (more if there will be annotations) and also increase the head or foot margin to accommodate running notes at the head or foot of the page. "Running" heads or feet run along the top or bottom of each page, identifying the chapter and section of text and the page number. Note also that inside margins must be wider to accommodate comb or spiral bindings and loose-leaf binders.

Flush Left versus Justified Text

Your next decision should be whether text will be flush left or justified. If you choose flush left, right margins will be ragged, and if you choose justified, line length will always be the same, and consequently right margins will be even. The pages in this book are justified, with only certain kinds of paragraphs (e.g., excerpts and examples) ragged right. Ragged right works best for informal text or short passages, while justified lines are needed for two-column text.

The drawback of justifying text is that the spaces between words in a line can appear so large or uneven as to distract the reader. Using hyphenation here and there at the ends of lines to eliminate large spaces between words also can lead to problems. While the ideal number of characters per line for avoiding excessive hyphenation is around 65, fewer characters per line may yield acceptable results.

Fonts Used

For typesetting textbooks and instructional materials, you would probably be wise to limit yourself to two fonts and their style variants, or three at the most. Include a serif font, such as New York, Garamond, or Times New Roman for typesetting text in paragraphs and a sans serif font, such as Helvetica or Arial for chapter titles, headings, and subheadings. You may also have a third font for special characters or special uses in design, such as figures, tables, and photo captions.

There are literally thousands of fonts. Many of them are copyright protected and must be licensed for a fee if you are planning to sell your projects. At the same time, many original fonts can be downloaded for free from the Internet. See the chapter appendix for more information.

Type Sizes and Leading

The point size of the characters used for typesetting paragraphs and the amount of spacing between lines within a paragraph and between paragraphs determines both the readability of the material and the amount that can be placed on a page. If the type is too small or the spacing between lines and paragraphs is too little, then the material will be difficult to read. On the other hand, if the type is too large or the spacing between lines and paragraphs are too great, the book or material takes up more pages and thus will cost more to print and also possibly will be irritating to read because of the need to turn pages frequently.

Unless you want to increase the number of pages in your book or material, you would be wise to select the smallest type size that is unlikely to affect readability adversely. Consider your audience. You could test for appropriate type size by setting a few pages in a particular point size and getting readers' opinions as to readability. Text type normally is set in the range from 9-point to 12-point type. The type sizes used for chapter titles and headings normally are larger, of course, than those used in paragraphs. In this book the text A-heads (main headings) are 14 points and the B-heads (subheadings) are 12 point bold italics.

Determining the appropriate amount of space between lines—or amount of leading—also can be done on a trial-and-error process. Without leading there would be practically no space between lines of text, making it effectively unreadable. In word processing programs the standard leadings are single space, one and one-half space, and double space, which can be increased or decreased by one or more points. Reducing the leading or other spacing on a page can make copy fit that otherwise would run over a line or two onto another page.

Design Principles to Apply

You would be wise to show sample pages of your textbook design to a professional designer. Design is an art and science. Williams (1994) has suggested four principles that if adhered to can enable even a novice to design visually attractive pages that facilitate communication. The first of these principles is *proximity*. According to Williams (1994, p. 14):

> Items relating to each other should be grouped close together. When several items are in close proximity to each other, they become one visual unit rather than several separate units. This helps organizing information and reducing clutter.

Headings and sub-headings, for example, should be in close enough proximity to the paragraphs to which they relate to form a single visual unit with them. According to the principle of *alignment* (Williams, 1994, p. 14):

> Nothing should be placed on the page arbitrarily. Every item should have a visual connection with something else on the page.

Unless there is a good reason for not doing so, all of the items on a page should be aligned the same way: flush left, flush right, centered, or justified. All of the lines on this page are justified, except quotes are ragged right.

The principle of *repetition*, according to Williams (1994, p. 14), states that you should:

Repeat visual elements of the design throughout the piece [e.g., book]. You can repeat color, shape, texture, spatial relationships, line thicknesses, sizes, etc. This helps develop the organization and strengthens the unity.

Examples of repeated elements in this book are the fonts used for typesetting paragraphs, headings, subheadings, chapter titles, and italicizing. Another repeated element is the amount of leading between lines, both within a paragraph and between paragraphs, and before and after headings.

In her principle of *contrast*, Williams states (1994, p.14) that you should:

Avoid elements on the page that are merely similar. If the elements (type, color, size, line thickness, shape, space, etc.) are not the same, make them very different. Contrast is often the most important visual attraction on a page.

Laying Out Text on Pages

When laying out text on pages for textbooks and instructional materials, you should, whenever possible, adhere to the design principles of proximity, alignment, repetition, and contrast. Perhaps the most helpful for laying out pages is referring to a textbook or instructional material the same trim size as yours with page designs that you like. A work that communicates similar material to a similar audience can serve as a model for laying out front matter—e.g., title page, copyright page, and table of contents—and indexes as well as chapters.

The layouts you use should not call attention to themselves. Readers should have little or no conscious awareness of them. They are a means to an end rather than an end in themselves. If they are effective, they will facilitate communicating what you intend your book or material to communicate.

If you do not want your book or material to be perceived as having been self-published, it is crucial that the text be laid out consistently from page to page and from chapter to chapter. Almost all sophisticated word processing and page layout programs enable you to define styles for automatically formatting specific text elements (e.g., chapter titles, quotations, headings, lists, etc.).

If your book or material consists entirely (or almost entirely) of text, you may want to consider doing typesetting and laying out pages while you are drafting. Doing so can save you time. This approach can also be used to lay out books and materials that contain more than a few illustrations, if you standardize the size and location of the space for illustrations on a page. The space for each illustration may be displayed on each page as either a frame (i.e., same-size rectangles or other shape) or the illustration itself.

You can indicate an illustration's location by temporarily inserting a rectangle that contains its number (e.g., "Figure 3.1"). Make the rectangle or frame the same height and width as the illustration with caption, or standardize the frame size to accommodate all your figures, tables, and photos. The rectangle is deleted when the illustration and caption are pasted in mechanically or digitally. The printer thus inserts the actual illustration into its place before printing.

Preparing Illustrations

Your textbook or instructional materials probably will contain at least a few illustrations. They may be graphs, drawings, or photographs, in black-and-white (monochrome) or color. As explained in Chapter 6, your responsibilities for illustrations—in addition to preparing pages to accept them—include securing illustrations by creating them yourself, contracting with someone to create them for you, or using existing photos and figures.

Creating Your Illustrations

The main requirement for drawings and photographs in textbooks and instructional materials is that they communicate clearly what you intend them to communicate. It is certainly desirable that they be of professional quality, but more important is their appropriateness, clarity, and pedagogical value. Fortunately, as mentioned earlier, graphics software is available that enables most users, even those with minimal artistic ability, to create serviceable figures and tables. In addition, drawing utilities enable most users to create illustrations that consist of interconnected, labeled, geometric forms, such as flow charts. Another type of illustration that you might be able to create yourself is a manipulation of an existing drawing or photo, which you can scan into your computer and modify. Recall that permissions may be needed to publish a modified illustration.

Finally, you may be able to create some of the photographs you need for illustrations. As discussed previously, a 35mm single-lens reflex, large format, or digital camera may be adequate for this purpose. As an example, I took many of the photographs for a textbook I authored, published by Allyn and Bacon in 1999, with a 1970s-model 35mm camera that I bought at a rummage sale for $25. Using software such as Adobe PhotoShop, a person with minimal artistic ability can modify photographs to improve their ability to communicate.

Commissioning Your Illustrations

You can contract with a photographer or artist to create illustrations. It is important that the contract between you and the artist or photographer be in the form of a work-for-hire agreement. This type of agreement specifies that the provider does not violate copyright, provides acceptable work at the agreed time for the agreed price, and transfers copyright of the work to you. Otherwise, the copyright for the illustration would belong to the photographer or artist, and you would have to obtain his or her permission to use it again.

The main disadvantage of contracting with an artist or photographer to create illustrations is that it can be very expensive to do so. You would be wise to get several estimates. The amount charged for creating a particular drawing or photograph can vary considerably. Original art for a cover may cost $500 to $1,500, while each graphical figure drawn from your sketch or specifications may cost $50 to $100.

Using Existing Drawings and Photographs

As explained in Chapter 6, if you find photographs or drawings that meet your needs—either as is or with modification—you may be able to obtain a copy and permission to reproduce it from its creator or publisher (depending on which of them owns the copyright). It is customary to charge a fee for such permissions, especially if you expect to sell your textbook or instructional material. However, you may be able to obtain permission for a nominal fee or for free if you indicate that your book or material will be used for "educational" or "nonprofit" purposes.

You may be able to obtain photographs or drawings from books and journals; government organizations, such as the Library of Congress; advertisements and catalogs; Web sites; disks and books containing clip art; and stock photo agencies. You usually can get permission from publishers to reproduce illustrations in books and journals and periodicals intended for the general public. Magazine illustrations can be expensive, however. In the 1980s, I paid $250 for permission to reproduce a cartoon from *The New Yorker Magazine*. Newspaper and wire service images also may be expensive. On the other hand, businesses usually are more than happy to let you use drawings and photographs from their advertisements and catalogs for free, so long as you clearly acknowledge their source. It is good free publicity for them! Free and low-cost illustrations also are available from some Web sites and from collections of clip art, which contain thousands of free generic drawings in the public domain. You simply cut and paste the art into your publication.

Stock photo and art agencies, however, are in business to sell reproduction rights to works created by professionals whom they represent. Some agencies have hundreds of thousands of photographs available on every imaginable subject. Photographs and art from these agencies tend to be expensive and are licensed for one-time use only. The cost depends on where the image will appear, the size of the image, and the number of books in which the image will be printed. An advantage of agencies is that they perform photo research for you and guarantee high quality.

Your other responsibilities for illustrations may include the following.

- Digitizing illustrations
- Modifying, cropping, and sizing illustrations
- Preparing halftones for illustrations

Digitizing and Modifying Illustrations

An illustration must be in digital form for it to be pasted into the computer file for a page of your book or material. If you don't have a digital file for an illustration that is compatible with your publishing software, you will have to create one using a scanner. The flat bed scanner is most commonly used now for digitizing both drawings and photographs. You place the sheet of paper containing the image to be digitized face down on the scanner's glass plate. The digitizer then divides the image into hundreds of thousands (perhaps millions) of tiny dots and then photographs and records in digital form the color of each dot. For a one-color line drawing without shading, there would be two possible values for each dot—one indicating black and one white. For a photograph, on the other hand, each dot would have more than two values. Consequently, image files for photographs (e.g., jpeg or tiff files) tend to be considerably larger than for simple graphs. Scanned illustrations can be compressed and saved on disk. Most photographic equipment dealers offer this service or can refer you to someone who does.

As previously noted, photographs and drawings can be modified onscreen. Parts can be erased, cropped, enlarged, or reduced. Text and graphic elements can be added, and elements from two or more images can be combined. Contrast, color, and sharpness of images also can be modified.

Preparing Halftones for Illustrations

Illustrations involving representational art and photographs will reproduce better if they are converted into halftones. A halftone version of a photograph or drawing consists of a series of tiny dots that vary in size and distribution. Examine a black-and-white photograph in a newspaper or magazine with a magnifying glass. You'll discover that the smaller and more dispersed the black dots are in an area, the lighter the shade of gray. Conversely, the larger and closer together the black dots are, the darker the shade of gray. Color photographs and drawings contain dots of the primary colors (cyan, yellow, magenta) and black. Each color dot is printed with a different plate, making four-color books more expensive to publish. Specific colors result from combining dots of the three colors in certain proportions, such as 20 percent yellow, ten percent cyan, and 5 percent black, for example.

Halftones can be created electronically and by a photographic process. The traditional method is to mount the photograph or art on a board and photograph it through a transparent screen that is etched with parallel lines both vertically and horizontally. The number of parallel lines per inch can be as low as 50 and as high as 200. When light pierces the thousands of tiny etched holes in the screen, tiny dots form on the film that vary in size and spacing depending on the shades and tones in the image. The greater the number of lines per inch, the higher the quality of the image. Unfortunately, the cost of the paper required to print 200-line-per-inch halftones is considerably higher than that required for 50-line-per-inch ones.

An alternative is software (such as Adobe PhotoShop) that

yields halftones comparable to those produced by the traditional photographic process. The image is scanned and processed to yield a dot configuration comparable to screened halftones having a particular number of lines per inch. You would be wise, however, to have your halftones made electronically by a printer. He or she can provide guidelines for preparing drawings and photographs from which the halftones will be made.

Preparing Captions

You also will need to write and place captions for your illustrations. One function of a caption is to link the illustration to which it is attached to the text content. Consequently, the caption for an illustration should provide such a link, in addition to furnishing information needed to interpret or communicate what it is intended. In addition, it is good practice to refer to figures and tables in the text narrative to provide a pedagogical context for viewing or studying them.

While captions usually are placed below the illustration, they can be placed at the side or above it. Captions can be centered or aligned with the illustration's left- or right-hand edge. If captions are left-aligned, the line length should neither exceed the width of the illustration nor be too short in relation to it. Ideally, lines should be the same width as, or a little shorter than, the illustration. Regardless of position or alignment, captions should be treated consistently throughout a publication.

Providing Your Master

Whether you are self-publishing on paper (camera-ready or typeset from disk) or electronically, your work will be reproduced from a master manuscript that you provide both in hardcopy and on disk. The pages of your master will be printed on sheets of a material (e.g., paper, film, or metal plates) or saved or burned onto a disk or uploaded onto a Web site.

If your book is being photographed camera ready and you want the pages to appear to have been professionally typeset, use at least a 600 dpi laser or inkjet printer. As explained previously, while a 600 dpi printer is likely to be adequate for camera-ready copy for pages that contain text and simple graphics, it is unlikely to be adequate for pages with halftones. For halftones, use a printer that can generate at least 1200 dpi.

Make certain that any computer used to print your pages has all of the necessary fonts. Otherwise, the computer may automatically substitute other fonts, which could result in incorrect characters and spacings. For example, the characters in a substituted font may be a little larger or smaller or a little narrower or wider than the ones generated by the intended fonts.

If your pages will be printed with a 300 dpi or 600 dpi printer, one way to increase the number of dots per inch is to print camera-ready copy larger than normal, and then have the printer reduce it to its correct size. This suggestion is most practical for books that will have a 5.5 x 8.5 or 6 x 9 trim size. Printers may or may not charge for making reductions.

When your book is ready to be published electronically, you may be asked to provide PDF files or to print the pages on paper and then have the pages scanned. As mentioned in Chapter 7, if your book is being published to a Web site, consider converting your files to PDF as read-only files that can be viewed using Acrobat Reader or MS Reader. After your book is in electronic form, it can be distributed by downloading it from the Internet or by making copies available on CDs. When your ebook or digital material is ready to be distributed, your master copy then can be duplicated.

Finally, before it goes to the printer, your master manuscript should be complete. That is, it should contain everything, including your front matter and back matter, which is the subject of the next chapter.

Online Resources for Preparing Pages

Typesetting Resources

Online source for free fonts: http://www.1001freefonts.com

True-Type, PostScript, Mac, and Windows fonts: http://www.fonts.com

Information on typography: http://www.planet-typography.com/directory/typo.html

Samples of point size, information on Web design: http://www.wpdfd.com/wpdtypo.htm

Web Style Guide on typography: http://www.webstyleguide.com/type/

Directory of typefaces: http://www.fontscape.com

Review of *The Mac Is Not a Typewriter* (2003): http://www.techsoc.com/macisnot.htm

Information on PDF and creating your own PDF files: http://searchpdf.adobe.com; http://www.searchtools.com/info/pdf.html, http://www.pdf995.com

Design Resources

Primer on book design: http://www.io.com/~hcexres/tcm1603/acchtml/book_design.html

Primer on page design: http://www.io.com/~hcexres/tcm1603/acchtml/page_design.html

Books on design for desktop publishers: http://www.newentrepreneur.com/Writer/Design_Book_Summary/design_book_summary.html

Design Tips for Layouts: http://desktoppub.about.com/library/tips/bldesigntips.htm

Reviews of *The Non-Designer's Design Book* and other books by R. Williams, such as *The PC Is Not a Typewriter:* http://www.programming-reviews.com/The_NonDesigners_Design_Book_1566091594.html

Examples of book page layouts: http://www.pneumabooks.com/intdesign.htm

Graphic design tutorials: http://desktoppub.about.com/cs/graphicdesign/

Yahoo directory for computer graphics software: http://dir.yahoo.com/Computers_and_Internet/Software/Graphics/

Examples and links for online freelance graphic designers: **http:// www.michaelgibbs.com/bottom_01links.html, http://www. dorriolds.com, http://www.illustrationboard.com**

Instructional design for Web site delivery: **http://edweb. sdsu.edu/clrit/learningtree/DCD/WWWInstrdesign/ WWWInstrDesign.html**

Principles of user-interface design: **http://www.sylvantech.com/ ~talin/projects/ui_design.html**

Tips on Web page layouts: **http://www.ncsu.edu/it/edu/online/ components/design_issues.html**

Illustration Resources

Adobe Illustrator: **http://www.adobe.com/products/illustrator/ main.html**

Cartoon Stock Directory: **http://www.cartoonstock.com**

Clip Art links page: **http://www.barrysclipart.com**

Public Domain Pictures: **http://www.princetonol.com/groups/iad/ links/clipart.html**

Public Domain Images for Multimedia Projects: **http://mciunix. mciu.k12.pa.us/~spjvweb/cfimages.html**

Understanding halftones: **http://www.designer-info.com/Writing/ understanding_halftones.htm**

Basics of color and black and white halftones: **http://desktoppub. about.com/library/weekly/aa090600a.htm**

Writing captions: **http://desktoppub.about.com/cs/pagelayout/ht/ captions.htm**

Model release forms: **http://www.dpcorner.com/all_about/releases. shtml**

Preparing Indexes and Front Matter

All textbooks require a title page, copyright page, table of contents, preface, and possibly other front matter. And all textbooks and professional books require references and an index. If you want libraries to acquire your reference work or nonfiction trade book, you likewise must provide an index and a bibliography. This chapter presents some guidelines for preparing front matter and back matter for your project (see also the chapter appendix).

Preparing Front Matter

Front matter consists of all the pages up to the first page of Chapter One and is usually numbered with lower-case Roman numerals. The front matter of a textbook can contain some or all of the following elements.

- Printed front endpapers
- Half-title page
- Frontispiece
- Title page
- Copyright page
- Dedication page
- Epigraph page
- Table of contents
- List of illustrations or figures
- Foreword
- Preface
- Acknowledgments
- Disclaimer

Printed Endpapers

The front endpapers of a textbook are the inside front cover and the page opposite it. They usually are left blank. However, information can be printed on the endpapers from which students can benefit—e.g., abbreviations, definitions of terms, formulae or measurements, or a map. The back endpapers can be printed with either the same information as on the front endpapers or with different information. Also, the endpapers may list special features of the textbook, such as topical boxes or cases.

Half-Title Page and Frontispiece

The half-title page is the first printed page of a book. It is found more often in hardbound books than in paperback ones. It contains only the title and is a right-hand page. The frontispiece is the left-hand page facing the title page. While it is usually left blank in textbooks, it can be used to list other books by the same author. In the history of book making the frontispiece originally was an engraved illustration, an ornament for the title.

Title Page and Copyright Page

The title page is on the right-hand side facing the frontispiece. It usually lists the full title and subtitle of the book; the name(s) of the author(s) or editor(s) and possibly also their titles and institutional affiliations; the publisher's name; and whether it is a first or revised edition. The copyright page is on the back of the title page. It is one of the pages in a book where a typographical error can have serious consequences. Proofread it carefully! It contains the copyright notice, the printing history (number of printings and revisions), the Library of Congress catalog number or control number, the ISBN, the Library of Congress Cataloging-in-Publication Data (CIP or PCIP), the name and address of the publisher (your company), and "Printed in the USA" (to avoid export complications).

Dedication Page and Epigraph Page

The dedication is on a right-hand page. You can dedicate your book to a group or class of people (e.g., "To my students, past and present") or to specific persons (e.g., to your mentor, parent, partner, spouse, and/or children). Only the person or persons mentioned are likely to be interested in your dedication. The epigraph page traditionally contains a pertinent quotation that sets the tone of the book. Most textbooks do not have an epigraph page, but may include epigraphs in the chapter opening pages.

Table of Contents and List of Illustrations

The table of contents should start on a right-hand page and include chapter numbers, titles, and beginning page numbers. It may also include major subheadings and their beginning page numbers. Front matter items such as a List of Illustrations, Preface, Acknowledgments, and Foreword also should appear on the contents page. Your table of contents is the main selling tool for your textbook or instructional material. By reading this front matter, potential adopters learn the scope, sequence, and theoretical or pedagogical orientation of your work. Thus, you would be wise to take care that your titles for parts and chapters and your headings and subheadings are clear and informative in expressing your book's content, organization, and mission. If your textbook is heavily illustrated or contains important pedagogy, you might include a list of illustrations or list of features at the end of the table of contents.

Foreword and Preface

The foreword is a pitch for a book and its author, written by one or more persons other than the author. It should begin on a right-hand page. This book has three forewords, but most books have one foreword by someone notable in the field the book covers. The name of the foreword's author helps to publicize and sell the book.

In your preface you should explain why you wrote the book and for whom and something about its content and organization. It is important that the preface is well written, because reviewers may base their reviews on it, rather than take the time to read every chapter. If you are writing a student textbook, the preface should address the students. In undergraduate textbooks it is common practice to include an instructor's preface followed by a student's preface to address the two different audiences. Your mission as an author and your objectives for your readers and your rationale for the content and organization of your book are appropriate subjects to include in a preface. Like the table of contents and foreword, the preface is a sales tool.

Acknowledgments and Disclaimer

In your acknowledgments list everyone who helped you with the book, including your editors and persons who reviewed prepublication drafts. It is particularly important to acknowledge contributors who are recognized as authorities in the field your textbook or instructional material covers. Their having vetted your book adds to its credibility. However, in commercial publishing it is important to have written permission to quote reviewers' remarks. If you are acknowledging only a few persons, you may want to do so in the Preface rather than having a separate Acknowledgments section.

Because of the possibility of someone being harmed by inaccurate information or inappropriate recommendations in your book, many authors include a disclaimer to partially protect themselves against litigation from this source. Poynter (1996, p.8) suggests a paragraph similar to the following:

> This book is designed to provide information in regard to the subject matter covered. It is sold with the understanding that the publisher and author are not engaged in rendering legal, accounting, or other professional services. If legal or other expert assistance is required, the services of a competent professional should be sought. The author and publisher shall have neither liability nor responsibility to any person or entity with respect to any loss or damage caused, or alleged to be caused, directly or indirectly by the information in this book.

See also the more succinct disclaimer on the copyright page of this book. Disclaimers can be appended to other front matter elements, such as the copyright page, rather than take up an extra whole page.

Indexing

In scholarly works, textbooks, professional trade books, and other academic materials, an index is essential. A good index helps the reader find critical information with minimum page turning and frustration. An index can be created by the author or by a professional indexer. If you index your book yourself, you might find the following general procedures helpful in developing the index.

- Identify the audience for whom you are writing the index.
- Identify valid (indexable) keywords (terms and concepts) for inclusion in index entries.
- Decide how to organize the information in your index and arrange your entries and subentries.
- Develop a style guide and format and apply them systematically throughout.
- Create and phrase index entries, including alternative terms.
- Bring together related information, cross-referencing appropriately.
- Create a usable index, and test it for usability.
- Edit for style, readability, content, accuracy, and space.

The chapter appendix offers leads to information about indexing software.

Wording and formatting index entries is a communication skill. You will need to decide whether to include gerunds, phrases beginning with prepositions, or guideword locators, for example, and whether to indent, run-in, or turn over lines. There also is more than one way to alphabetize an index. The more you decide in advance, the smoother your indexing process will go as you work page by page.

For example, decide in advance what classes of information to include or exclude. Will you include or exclude place names, author names, acronyms, abbreviations, or numerical references in your index? Will you include key terms and phrases from your headings and captions? How much will you differentiate within and between terms and concepts? Will your index be too thin or too dense? How much information is enough? Your choices for what to include and exclude should be based on what your readers are likely to need or want to know and what vocabulary they are likely to use to try to locate this information in your book.

Two kinds of indexes for textbooks are author indexes and subject indexes. You may or may not want to prepare an author index in addition to a subject index. In some content areas an author index might increase adoptions. If you cite the research and publications of the instructors who teaches the course, they might be more likely to adopt it. Instructors naturally would like their students to be aware of their professional work and, consequently tend to react favorably to a textbook in which their work is mentioned.

Indexing Software

There is special software for indexing. The American Society of Indexers' publication, *Software for Indexing* (Schroeder, 2003) evaluates programs available for PCs and Macs. Also, most word processing programs have the capability to generate an index. In addition, any word processing program that has a "Find" command can be used. The first time you refer to an item, you enter it into an index file at the appropriate point alphabetically. Whenever you want to refer to it again, you use the "Find" function to locate it quickly. I have indexed seven textbooks in this simple way.

If your book is not a first edition, the index from the current edition can be quite useful for indexing, particularly if you have it on your hard drive or on disk. Your first task is to delete items in the index that are not relevant to or accurate for the new edition, including page numbers. I have used my word processor's "Find and Replace" command to delete page numbers efficiently. I simply ask the program to "Find" each of the ten digits from 0 to 9 and to "Replace" each digit with nothing—i.e., leaving the "Replace" entry space blank. After issuing the "Find and Replace" command 10 times, once for each of the 10 digits, there would remain a series of commas after each item in the index, with each comma separated from the next by a space. To delete these commas and spaces, use the "Find and Replace" command to locate each instance of "space comma" and leave the "Replace" space blank. This process usually takes less than 30 minutes.

The use of the automatic indexing capability of word processing programs has a serious limitation if the numbering of the pages in the manuscript does not conform exactly to the numbering of the book pages (called folios). It is difficult to make the number of characters on manuscript pages correspond to book pages unless you are preparing camera-ready pages using the same program you used to draft the manuscript. In commercial textbook publishing accurate indexes are created from final page proof after it is certain that folios will not change.

Indexing Help

The quality of your textbook's index can significantly affect its acceptance and sales. It takes time to develop a good index, and you can arrange to have your book indexed by a freelance indexer. Most professional indexers charge between $1.50 and $3.00 per page, as they read every page to construct the index. Alternatively, indexers may charge $.50 to $.75 per index entry. It is crucial to find an indexer who is knowledgeable about the topics in your book.

There are several ways to search for a competent freelance indexer. One is to seek recommendations from other self-publishers. A second is to seek recommendations from a university press at your institution or another. And a third is to search the American Society of Indexers' Web site (**www.asindexing.org/site/**) for its ASI Indexer Locator. The Locator can be accessed from the Society's Web site and contains a listing and description of the experience of many freelance indexers.

Preparing Other Back Matter

Other than an index, textbooks and instructional materials typically have endnotes or references and a bibliography. That is, it is expected that, other than having a subject index and possibly an author index, textbooks and instructional materials will cite sources and thus will need end notes or references and a bibliography in the back matter. Endnotes for parenthetical source citations may be gathered at the back of the book by chapter, or may be given at the ends of the chapters in which they appear. Source citations also may appear in footnotes, but footnotes are reserved for scholarly works rather than textbooks. Note also that footnotes greatly increase production and manufacturing costs on a per-page basis, because they require selective manual override in printing outside of the text block.

In contrast to endnotes, references comprise a single alphabetical list of all the sources you cited or referred to, and these, too, can be gathered as chapter end matter or as book end matter. Bibliographies, on the other hand, include all the works that you consulted in writing your book, whether or not you had occasion to cite them specifically. In student textbooks, special annotated bibliographies in the chapter end matter might suggest specific readings for students.

Student textbooks also often have one or more appendices and a glossary in the back matter. These are pedagogical tools to enhance text content and aid learning. In many undergraduate textbooks, key terms and concepts are boldfaced in the chapter narrative and then defined in an end-of-book glossary. These elements, like other back matter, may be presented alternatively as chapter end matter. The usual sequence of back matter, following the book's conclusion or epilogue, is Appendix, Glossary, Notes, References, Bibliography, Author Index, and Subject Index.

Robust glossaries, references, and bibliographies are important resources for students and also serve as another checkpoint for instructors when they make decisions about course adoptions. Whichever end matter and back matter elements you use, you should consistently follow the academic style you have chosen for formatting them. As examples of treatments of front matter and back matter elements, see the front matter and back matter of this book.

Online Resources for Preparing Front Matter and Back Matter

Front matter and back matter information, including page impositions: **http://www.hodi.com/book_front-back_matter. html**

How to prepare front and back matter: **http://saulcarliner.home. att.net/id/bookelements.htm**

Examples of model prefaces: **http://www.ickn.org/elements/ hyper/cyb1.htm, http://www.webstyleguide.com/front/ preface-1.html**

Bibliography Styles: **http://www.english.uiuc.edu/cws/ wworkshop/bibliography.htm**

Examples of Glossary Styles (online glossaries of writing and publishing terms): **http://www.umuc.edu/prog/ugp/ ewp_writingcenter/writinggde/glossary/glossary-01.shtml, http://txtx.essortment.com/writingwriterg_rffv.htm, http:// freelancewrite.about.com/library/glossary/blglossary.htm**

Indexing Resources on the Web: **http://www.slais.ubc.ca/ resources/indexing/software.htm#bob**

American Society of Indexers on Indexing: **http://www. asindexing.org/site/indfaq.shtml**

American Society of Indexers on Indexing Software: **http://www. asindexing.org/site/software.shtml**

wINDEX: **http://www.abbington.com/holbert/windex.html**

Web Site Indexing Software: **http://www.software-programs.net/ indexing_software/indexing_software.html**

Software for Indexing: **http://www.anindexer.com/about/sw/ swindex.html**

Best Practices in Indexing: **http://www.wordsmith.co.il/seminar2. html**

10 Copyrighting and Registering
a Self-Published Work

Any book or material that you author—whether it is published on paper, disks, CD, tape, or the Internet—is considered nationally and internationally as your property (i.e., intellectual property). To qualify for copyright protection, a work must be original and must exist in a concrete medium of expression. This includes performances, for example, as well as books, tapes, and other media. The law by which your ownership rights are protected in the United States is the Copyright Act of 1976 and its amendments. It is desirable, but usually not essential, to get formal copyright protection by registering books and materials that you self-publish with the U.S. Copyright Office. In addition to registering your self-published work with the Copyright Office, it is desirable that you register them with several other agencies. These include the agency that assigns ISBNs for books (and ISSNs for periodicals) as well as the Cataloging Department of the Library of Congress.

Copyrighting Books and Materials

Our government has recognized since its inception that authors should be allowed to profit from their creations. The source of this recognition appears to have been "natural law," which views it as only fair that authors be granted the exclusive right to benefit from their creations for a specific period of time. The framers of the Constitution felt so strongly about the need to protect the right of authors to profit from their creations that they gave Congress the following power in Article 1, Section 8, of the U.S. Constitution:

Congress shall have the power...to promote the progress of science and useful arts, by securing for limited times to authors and inventors the exclusive right to their respective writings and discoveries.

The mechanisms that Congress created to protect these rights were the copyright and the patent. A copyright is the right to copy an author's work. The person owning the copyright, who may or may not be the author, has the exclusive right for a specified period of time to make and sell copies of the work; consequently, he or she holds the copyright for the work. The work may be perceivable by vision, audition, touch, or some combination of the three.

Copyright laws have two basic objectives, both of which can be inferred from Article 1, Section 8. The first objective "is to foster the creation and dissemination of intellectual works for the public welfare" (Dible, 1978, p. 115). These laws "foster the creation and dissemination of intellectual works" by giving the person who publishes them (who may or may not be their author) the opportunity to recoup expenses and possibly make a profit. Copyright owners do this by making it unlawful for anyone else to make copies of the work for sale during the term of the copyright. If there were no copyright laws, you would be hesitant to invest the money necessary to publish a book or material, because someone else could make copies of it and possibly sell them at a lower price.

The second objective of copyright laws "is to give the creators the reward due them for their contribution to society" (Dible, 1978, p. 115). The laws do this in two ways: first, by requiring anyone who copies part of an author's work to get permission to do so and to cite the source by indicating the title of the work and the name of its author, and second, by protecting the author's right to profit financially from the sale of copies of his or her works. No one is permitted to duplicate and sell copies of an author's work for the duration of the copyright without the owner's permission.

Provisions of Copyright Law

The Copyright Act of 1976 (Public Law 94-553) was the first general revision of U.S. copyright law since 1909. The Act became fully effective on January 1, 1978. This discussion is limited to aspects of the Act likely to be relevant to the activities of self-publishers. The order in which topics are discussed corresponds roughly to the order in which they are mentioned in the statute. The primary sources for this discussion are Dible, 1978 (pp. 111-254) and the Cornell University online law library, which includes updates since 1978 and court cases concerning copyright law.

Duration of Copyright Protection

For works of authorship created after January 1, 1978, the duration of copyright protection is the life of the author plus seventy years after his or her death. For works of more than one author, the fifty-year period is measured from the date of the death of the last surviving author. Copyrights that are renewed (called subsisting copyrights) are granted for periods of 67 years. Any copyright owner can renew including the beneficiaries or heirs of deceased authors. All copyrights run through December 31 of the calendar year in which they expire.

Material That Can Be Copyrighted

The 1976 Copyright Act substitutes the phrase "original works of authorship" for "writings of an author" when designating the type of material that can be copyrighted. Thus, original works of authorship that can be copyrighted are not limited to those containing written words (referred to in the statute as "literary works"). Original works also include: (1) pictorial and graphic works, (2) motion pictures and other audiovisual works, (3) sound recordings, and (4) computer and multimedia programs.

The category of literary works includes any works expressed in "words, numbers, or other verbal or numerical symbols or indicia." While a literary work has to be original in the sense of not being merely a copy of a preexisting work, there is no requirement that it be novel or ingenious, or that it possess aesthetic merit. The category of pictorial and graphic works includes photographs and drawings. Like literary works, photographs and drawings must be original in the sense of not being merely copies of preexisting images, but, again, their novelty, ingenuity, or aesthetic merit are not considerations in determining whether they can be copyrighted.

The category of motion pictures and other audiovisual works includes films, videotapes, and DVDs; and the category of sound recordings includes phonograph records, audiotapes, compact disks

(CDs), and digital audiotape (DAT) cartridges. The category of computer programs includes both the codes of which programs are comprised and the audiovisual displays and digital content that the codes produce. The two forms may be copyrighted separately because substantially the same audiovisual effect can be achieved by different sets of computer code.

What cannot be copyrighted? There are six types of materials mentioned in the Act that are denied U.S. copyright protection, of which three are likely to be of particular interest to self-publishers. For example, ideas, methods, systems, and principles cannot be copyrighted. One of the fundamental principles promulgated by law is that "copyright does not protect ideas, methods, systems, principles, etc. but rather the particular manner in which they are expressed or described" (Dible, 1978, p. 127). Consequently, for example, a copyright does not protect a clinician's ideas or methods from being copied; it only protects the particular arrangement of words in which he or she expresses or describes them.

Other types of subject matter denied U.S. copyright protection are blank forms and raw data. According to Dible (1978, p. 127), "Blank forms and similar works designed to record rather than convey information, are not subject to copyright protection." Some of the forms used for recording client's responses to psychological tests probably are not protected by copyright for this reason, even though a copyright notice is printed on them. Anyone can place a copyright notice on any work he or she creates, whether or not it is copyrightable by law. The copyright notice (©) on an uncopyrightable blank form tends to discourage others from copying it, simply because most people are not sufficiently familiar with copyright law to know that it cannot be copyrighted. Likewise, raw data is in the public domain.

A third type of subject matter denied U.S. copyright protection is most works of the U.S. government. According to Dible (1978, p. 128), "works produced for the U.S. Government by its officers and employees as a part of their official duties are not subject to U.S. copyright protection." This category does not necessarily include works prepared by researchers or scholars under a U.S. government contract or grant. The funding agency decides whether an independent contractor or grantee will be allowed to copyright works supported wholly or partially by government funds.

Ownership and Transfer of Rights

The author of a work that was not prepared within the scope of his or her employment is the owner of the copyright, unless he or she transfers ownership to somebody else. If such a work has more than one author, the co-authors jointly own the copyright unless or until they transfer it to somebody else, such as a publisher.

The copyright to a "work prepared by an employee within the scope of his or her employment" belongs to the employer, unless the employer transfers it to the employee in writing. Such a work is referred to in the Copyright Act as a work made for hire. "The rationale for this rule is that the work is produced under the employer's direction and expense; also the employer bears the risks and should be allowed to reap the benefits" (Dible, 1978, p. 130). However, your employer would not be entitled to the own a work you authored that you prepared outside the scope of your employment. If you plan to author a work from which you plan to profit, and if you do this wholly or partially while on the job or at your employer's expense, then your employer may feel entitled to own the copyright. To avoid a misunderstanding, it might be a good idea before beginning a work to request a letter from your employer acknowledging your right to copyright the work in your name (or, if your employer contributes significantly to the creation of it, in both your names). Another way to avoid a misunderstanding is to work on the project at home on your own time. Colleges and universities usually have stated policies regarding the authoring activities of their faculty members.

Reproduction and Fair Use

It is not always necessary to secure written permission to reproduce text. The Copyright Act of 1976 places certain restrictions on prohibiting the reproduction of copyrighted materials. One such restriction is referred to as the doctrine of "fair use"— a component of the Copyright Act of 1976. This doctrine allows copying without permission from or payment to the copyright owner when the use is "reasonable and not harmful to the rights of the copyright owner"(Dible, 1978, p. 142). While Section 107 of the Act, which deals with fair use, seems somewhat vague, it uses the following four guidelines for deciding when the "fair use" rule is applicable.

1. Purpose and character of the use, including whether such use is commercial or for nonprofit educational

purposes
2. Nature of the copyrighted work
3. Amount and substantiality of the portion used in relation to the copyrighted work as a whole
4. Effects of the use on the potential market for the copyrighted work or on its value

In the first guideline, the courts tend to define fair use liberally for nonprofit works for educational uses. Commercial textbook publishing is a multi-billion dollar industry, however, and although the works are for educational purposes, they may be just as vulnerable to copyright infringement suits as trade books.

In the second guideline, the courts tend to define fair use conservatively for copyrighted works that are not professional or academic books or journals. Consequently, it probably is a good idea to get written permission before quoting even a few lines of text from a publication that is not a professional or academic one. When quoting poetry, for example, permission is needed even for only a single line.

The third guideline is one of the two most important determiners of a court's decision about the applicability of the fair use doctrine. Quoting more than a line or two from a very short work, or five percent or more from a work less than book length, definitely requires written permission. While there isn't general agreement among specialists on copyright law on the amount that it is safe to quote from a book length work without written permission, many publishers will risk up to 500 words.

The final fair use guideline—the impact that the use is likely to have on sales of the work—is the other crucial determiner of applicability. Would your use of the material diminish the value of the source or reduce the copyright owner's sales? A court likely would consider it far-fetched for the publisher of a professional or scientific journal to claim that quoting 200 words from an article reduced sales of the journal. On the other hand, if chapters of a book were copied without permission for classroom use, the situation would be entirely different. A court likely would be sympathetic to the idea that the copying of chapters for this purpose resulted in a loss of sales for the book.

Notice of Copyright

It is desirable that you place a copyright notice on all works for which you want copyright protection. The notice should contain the following three elements (Dible, 1978, pp. 228-229).

1. Symbol © (the letter C in a circle), or the word "Copyright"
2. Year of the first publication of the work
3. Name(s) of the owner(s) of the copyright in the work, or an abbreviation or symbol by which the name(s) can be recognized

According to the U.S. Copyright Office, you should register your published work within three years after publication. As mentioned previously, formal application for a copyright is not a prerequisite for placing a copyright notice on your work or for actual copyright protection. Your original work is protected as soon as it is in concrete form, and the mere placement of a copyright notice on a work ordinarily is sufficient to discourage persons from copying it without permission. The formal registration of a copyright, however, does increase the number and types of remedies that you or your publisher could seek from a court in the event of infringement.

Depositing

The formal copyrighting of a work ordinarily involves (1) depositing two complete copies in the Library of Congress and (2) completing an application for copyright registration and paying the required fee ($30 as of this printing). Exceptions to the requirement to deposit two copies of the work in the Library of Congress include (1) if fewer than five copies of the work have been published, or (2) the work is an expensive limited edition with numbered copies for which the requirement to deposit two copies could be regarded as burdensome, unfair, or unreasonable (see Section 407C of the 1976 Copyright Act).

Copyright Infringement and Remedies

Owners of a copyright can seek several types of legal remedies if the copyright is infringed. They can ask a court to issue an injunction or restraining order that will temporarily or permanently prevent or stop infringements. They can ask a court to impound all allegedly infringing copies of the work during the time a suit for infringement is pending. They can ask a court to award compensatory damages, which would offset the profits they lost because of the sale of the infringer's copies. Or they can ask a court to award them statutory damages, which are a type of punitive damages that defendants can be required to pay simply because they infringed the plaintiff's copyright. They are referred to as "statutory" damages because they are specified in the statute, or law. The owners of a copyright may, of course, decide against seeking a remedy from a court for their copyright being infringed because litigation is time consuming, energy draining, and expensive.

These remedies may extend to unauthorized uses of your work in other countries. In 1989 the U.S. joined the Berne Convention for the Protection of Literary and Artistic Works, which includes the writings of scholars, academic authors, and textbook writers. Other conventions and treaties include the Universal Copyright Convention, special provisions of GATT 1994, and others.

Other Registrations

If your project is a textbook or academic material, there are two other registrations for which you should apply, as mentioned earlier. These registrations include the following.

- An International Standard Book Number (ISBN) or International Standard Serial Number (ISSN) if your work is a periodical, and
- A Library of Congress Catalog Card Number or Library of Congress Control Number (LCCN).

You should print both numbers on the copyright page of your textbook or academic material. You also should have the ISBN printed in a bar code format on the back cover of the book. Your printer should be able to arrange to have a mechanical, digital file, or film made for the bar code, or you can send away for a bar code yourself through firms that provide this service. Information about applying for an ISBN, bar code, LCCN, and Cataloging in Publication (CIP, PCIP) data is given in Chapter 5. Libraries, college bookstores, and academic book wholesalers and distributors are unlikely to carry your book if it lacks these identifying numbers.

Granting Permission to Use Your Work

Making your audience aware of the availability of your properly identified work is the subject of Chapter 11. In any event, just as you request permission to use others' materials in your work, members of your audience who become authors may seek permission to include your material in their work. This use is not regarded as a subsidiary right but falls under the provisions of copyright law. If you decide to give permission, you can provide the material gratis or charge a fee. Publishers, including self-publishers, are more likely to charge a permission fee when the publication in which the material will be reprinted is expected to generate significant income.

If you are willing to grant permission, the fee you ask for must be reasonable. As a rule of thumb, for a journal article, professional journals typically charge $25 to $50 per page. If you wish to request a higher permission fee, you probably would be wise to negotiate it. When you grant permission, be sure to specify the type of use, the extent or distribution of the use right (U.S. only, U.S. and Canada, World), the duration of the use right (first edition only, first and second editions, all editions), and a language restriction (English only, English and Japanese, etc.). Foreign language rights and translation rights for all or part of a book-length work are subsidiary rights and should be negotiated separately from use permissions. Subsidiary rights are the subjects of Chapter 13.

Online Resources for Copyrighting and Registering a Work

U.S. Copyright Office: http://www.loc.gov/copyright
Form TX: http://www.loc.gov/copyright/forms
Copyright Act of 1976 (PL 94-553) and Information on
Copyright Law: http://www.law.cornell.edu/topics/copyright.html
ISBNs and ISSNs: http://www.isbn.org, http://www.issn.org
Bar Codes: http://www.mecsw.com/specs/bookland.html
Copyright Clearance Center: http://www.authors.copyright.com
Information on Copyright and Examples of Permissions Forms:
http://www.lib.ncsu.edu/scc/contents.html
Help for Authors on Copyright Issues: http://www.authorsguild.org, http://www.TAAonline.net
Library of Congress Preassigned Control Numbers (PCN), to get
an LCCN: http://pcn.loc.gov/pcn
Cataloging in Publication (CIP): http://cip.loc.gov/cip
Sources for Publisher's Cataloging in Publication (PCIP): http://www.dgiinc.com, http://www.qualitybooks.com

11

Practical Marketing Approaches for Academic Self-Publishers

Marketing actually begins well before you have your book in print. If a sizable percentage of the students and their instructors who could benefit from your textbook or instructional material are unaware that they exist, you are unlikely to sell enough copies even to recover your expenses. And, perhaps more importantly, students and instructors or others who could use the information to help themselves will not be able to do so. Thus, from the very beginning you will need to develop strategies for marketing your publications.

One reason not to self-publish a book or material is if you have what Judith Applebaum (1988) refers to as "fear of hustling." This fear stems from the belief that it is not dignified or academically respectable to promote yourself or your creations. If you suffer from this attitude, you probably will not market your textbook or instructional material adequately enough to be successful. However if you self-publish a work that you regard as potentially helpful to at least a small group of people, and if the price they would have to pay for copies is fair, then there is no question that aggressively marketing your work is academically respectable. The people who can be helped by it or can utilize the information must be aware that it exists! If you cannot accept at a gut level that aggressively marketing your work is academically respectable, then you should not self-publish. Alternatively, you should be prepared to invest in the services of a publicist or marketing consultant or to turn over your publication to an exclusive distributor who will handle marketing for you. See the chapter appendix for more information.

Marketing options for self-publishers of textbooks and instructional materials include any combination of the following approaches.

- Foreword written by a notable contributor
- Endorsements from peer reviewers and adopters
- Announcements in professional circles
- Press releases
- Reviews in key publications
- Directory listings
- Articles and interviews citing your book or material
- Presentation and representation at professional meetings
- Examination copies
- Direct-mail marketing
- Networking and Telemarketing
- Direct selling from your Web site
- Working with distributors and wholesalers
- Marketing to academic libraries
- Marketing to bookstores
- Amazon.com and Barnesandnoble.com
- E-mail promotions
- Advertising
- Radio and television promotions
- Book signings
- Workshops based on your book or material

This list of marketing approaches may seem intimidating. However, each approach can be grouped into a practical sequence of four general marketing initiatives: your first steps in getting the word out, further developing your marketing campaign, working with wholesalers and distributors, and developing special promotions. This chapter is organized in terms of these four areas.

Your First Steps

Marketing and promotion can become overwhelming in scope as well as cost in time and money. Next to the cost of printing, marketing is likely to be your biggest expense. You would be wise to begin with basic measures in familiar areas, such as arranging to have a foreword written for your book and making sure it gets listed in key publisher directories.

A Foreword

The purpose of a foreword is to enhance a book's credibility. Thus, a person who writes the foreword is someone whom many potential adopters and purchasers of the book would recognize and accept as an authority in the field. A book can have more than one foreword. This book has three, though this is not usual! Whatever the number, forewords should contribute to both setting the material in an appropriate context and enhancing its credibility. Announce the author of the foreword on the cover of your book.

Endorsements

The purpose of an endorsement, like that of a foreword, is to enhance a book's credibility. Endorsements from persons who are likely to be regarded as authorities in the field your book addresses can increase both course adoptions and individual sales. It is academically respectable to include endorsements on the back cover of the book, in the front matter, in packaging, and in materials for marketing and promotion, such as brochures.

The best way to get endorsements is to ask for them. It is academically respectable to do so if you do not offer to pay for them. Contact authorities in the field and ask them if they would be willing to review the manuscript and, if they like it, write an endorsement that you can quote. If your textbook or instructional material really is good, readers who want to be considered authorities might jump at the chance to endorse it. Being chosen to endorse a book often is interpreted as a sign that the endorser is nationally or internationally known and respected as an authority or expert.

Another kind of endorsement important to get is testimonials of prospective or actual adopters or users of your work. This form of peer review is crucial to your success as an educational self-publisher. Quite often, the decision of whether to review your work in a professional or industry journal is based on preexisting peer and user reviews as well as endorsements. In addition, you can use critical peer reviews as you revise, to develop and refine your work for your intended readers.

Press Releases

Press releases (or news releases) enable you to get free publicity for your book or material. Essentially, you send stories to news media in addition to professional associations to announce publication and generate interest in your product. There are standard formats for news releases, which should link your book or material to news of the day or to professional issues in some way. In other words, your book should be newsworthy, or it should solve a problem of interest to readers of the publication in which your press release will appear.

In journalism, making your story relevant is called having an "angle" or a "hook." For example, you might present the founding of your publishing company in local or regional newspapers in relation to local or regional business news. You might present your textbook in criminal justice in relation to the context of recent changes in the criminal justice system brought about by Homeland Security. You might write a timely story about your literature anthology that ties it in to National African American Literature Week. Or you might discuss your work in relation to your response to a debate in the journal or newsletter of your professional association.

Announcements

Your press release can be the basis of announcements to colleagues in your professional circles. Many journals, newsletters, and alumni magazines print announcements of recently published textbooks and instructional materials. The announcement may be limited to a listing in a publication's "books and materials received" column. Or it may include a paragraph in which the book or material is described and ordering information is provided. Your chances of getting an announcement with paragraph are enhanced if you draft a press release and submit it to the editor along with a copy of your book or material. Editors appreciate having material submitted to them that they can print almost as is. Also inform them that you can send image files (jpeg or tiff files) of the cover the book and a portrait of the author. Print mass media tend to be picture-based.

Depending on the nature of your book or material, it may make sense to send a copy of your press release to the editor of the alumni magazine at your institution and to the editors of the alumni magazines at the institutions from which you graduated. Some of your past students or colleagues may buy copies. Also consider donating a copy to the library of your alma mater.

Reviews

Review copies of your self-published textbook or instructional material should be sent to the editor of journals and newsletters that have relevant content. Editors may be willing to review your work or to publish a review written by someone else. You may also want to send review copies to publications not associated with your profession, such as local news or book review magazines and college alumni magazines. Because sales of your textbook will depend in large part on word of mouth, reviews in publications are important sources of publicity.

It is crucial at first to appear to be a small press rather than a self-publisher. Many industry reviewers avoid reviewing self-published textbooks and instructional materials. The mailing label and stationery you use should be printed with the letterhead of your publishing company, and the language you use in the cover letter should be comparable to that of other textbook publishers.

If your book is appropriate for acquisition by college and university libraries, a publication to which you should definitely send your finished book is *CHOICE*. This journal, published eleven times a year by American Library Association, is one of the main sources that college and university librarians consult when making acquisition decisions. While only about a third of the books *CHOICE* receives each year are reviewed, a good review in it is likely to yield sales. See the chapter appendix for other sources of prepublication and post-publication reviews.

Directory Listings

You can have your book listed for free in various print and online directories and bibliographies for publishers and for publications. It is especially important to have your self-published textbooks listed in *Books in Print*, because this is the main reference used by bookstores and libraries in the United States for identifying books that have been published. It is updated frequently and published in both print and electronic editions. Listings include all the information needed for ordering, including ISBNs and mailing addresses of publishers. When you activate an ISBN number for a textbook by completing and submitting an Advanced Book Information (ABI) form included in the packet you receive from R.R. Bowker (see Chapter 5), you both register your textbook and get it listed in *Books in Print* at no charge. Listing your textbooks and the name of your publishing company in *Books in Print* also has the benefit of further persuading potential customers that you are not a vanity press. See the appendix for more information on directories.

Developing Your Marketing Campaign

Once you have requested a foreword, written a press release, arranged for announcements, received endorsements, requested reviews, and applied for listings in directories, you are ready to go more deeply into the marketing process. Marketing is ongoing and does not end; one campaign simply succeeds another as you explore each avenue for reaching your customers.

Articles and Interviews

A good way to generate interest in your textbook or instructional material is to write articles based on it or related to it and to submit these articles to publications that your prospective customers are likely to read. Articles by others who cite your work also help to get the word out, as are articles about you or interviews in which your publications are mentioned. If possible, include information on how copies can be ordered. Also remember to request copies of these published articles (called tearsheets) for your publicity kit.

You can make use of articles and interviews in several ways aside from your publicity kit. Local, regional, or professional media might be interested in publishing an interview of you in which your publications are mentioned. Or you might publish a few chapter-based articles on your Web site or another, or link to or from articles about you or your book on your Web site. If you write an article for a professional journal on a subject related to your book, mention the title, publisher, and ISBN in the biographical sketch that typically follows such an article.

Presenting and Exhibiting

Your local public or university library might be interested in sponsoring a talk you give in which you can refer to your publication. You also might present at local, regional, and national conventions and conferences or meetings of professional associations on topics that your textbook covers in depth, and include information about your publication in a handout. You also may want to take some books with you to the professional meetings, conferences, and conventions that you attend, particularly ones at which you will be presenting. It may be possible to sell your book or material yourself or to have someone else do so. Or this may be a convenient way to distribute review copies.

If there is a commercial exhibit area at your meeting, you may want to have a booth at which your publications are displayed or made available for purchase. An alternative to having your own booth is having your textbook or instructional material displayed by an exhibiting service, such as Association Book Exhibit (ABE), if the service has a booth at a relevant conference or convention. Marketing associations for small publishers, such as Publishers Marketing Association (PMA) also have cooperative booths for their members at various conventions associated with academic publishing.

Sending Examination Copies

It is common practice in college textbook publishing to give examination copies of student textbooks to instructors of courses for which they are likely to be appropriate. Examination copies can be sent to all instructors who teach a particular course or only to those who request them. You would send a flyer or brochure to—or otherwise contact—instructors who teach the course for which you have written, describing your publication and offering an examination copy. You could allow those who receive an examination copy to keep it whether or not they adopt the book, or you could make keeping a free copy contingent on adoption. If the latter, be sure to indicate that if the recipient does not adopt the book, he or she should either return or pay for it.

Sending out a large number of examination copies of textbooks to potential adopters can have two undesirable consequences. First, the cost of printing and mailing them can be prohibitive. And second, it can reduce income by increasing the number of used copies on the market. Instructors sell examination copies of textbooks to secondhand textbook wholesalers, even though doing so is unethical. You would be wise, therefore, to distribute examination copies to instructors selectively to those who profess to have a strong interest in considering your book for adoption.

Direct Mail Marketing

Textbooks and instructional materials are marketed through direct mailing of promotional material to intended customers. You mail brochures with order blanks to people for whom your book or material is likely to be useful. Brochures used for direct mail marketing list the ways that recipients are likely to benefit by purchasing the book or material. The second most important copy in the brochure is information about the content.

For both direct mail marketing and other publicity efforts, you definitely should turn out a brochure or flyer for your textbook or instructional material that contains an order blank. The brochure type commonly used is two pages, printed on both sides of a sheet of 8.5 x 11 paper. The brochure should contain a brief description of the book, a list of benefits from using it, a list of chapter contents, a paragraph about you that establishes your credibility as the author, and brief excerpts from reviews and endorsements.

The persons to whom textbooks and instructional materials are marketed by direct mail are teachers or college instructors who are members of educational, academic, professional, or scientific institutions or associations. Almost all associations sell their membership lists. It may even be possible to purchase a segment of a mailing list (e.g., instructors who teach a particular course). Commercial data retrieval houses also rent mailing lists or supply mailing labels for one-time use based on your category selections. The cost for this service typically is between $75 and $100 per one thousand names. See the appendix for more information about mailing lists.

You will find that postage, along with printing, are the biggest costs of marketing. Thus, it would be worth you time and effort to find the most efficient and economical ways to do mass mailings, as well as the best rates. You might find the flat rate priority mail envelope or media mail or UPS ground to be the best for sending examination copies of your book. Postcard houses might offer discounted bulk mailing rates. You might defray postage through a cooperative mailing with another publisher. You might be able to mail your flyer or brochure at less expense if it weighs less (e.g., is printed on 50-pound opaque paper rather than regular stock).

Be forewarned that responses to direct mail marketing can be disappointing, as little as 1 or 2 percent. As indispensable as it is for getting the word out to prospective adopters, direct mail alone is not sufficient to make your marketing campaign a success. This reality must be balanced against your budget for bringing you book to market in relation to its sales price.

Telemarketing

You can use a telephone several ways to facilitate marketing college textbooks. You can, for example, establish a toll-free number for order taking. Most publishers have them. To use one effectively for order taking, you must be able to accept credit cards, which means you must acquire merchant card services. If you do not want to have an in-house 800 line, you can sign up with a toll-free answering service or a toll-free virtual fax service that comes to you as email via your phone line. However you take phone orders, you should prepare a standard script or have a standard order form on which to record information.

In addition to using telemarketing for passive order taking, you can use it to facilitate sales through networking. For example, you can phone colleagues and instructors of courses for which your textbook would be appropriate and ask if they would like an examination copy or would be interested in reviewing it. If they request one, you could phone them again to verify that the book has arrived, inquire if they have any questions, and determine if they are interested in adopting it. You can repeat a similar process for each new edition you self-publish. Note, however, that today "Do Not Call" ordinances in many states restrict commercial mass telemarketers, so you would be wise to use the phone for specific contacts that you have researched.

Marketing on Your Web Site

Most publishers, even very small ones, have Web sites for both promoting and selling their books and materials. Their products can be ordered online directly from their Web site as well as from Internet bookstores (e.g., Amazon.com and Barnes & Noble) to which their Web site is linked. You will need a Web host, shopping cart, and merchant card service for conducting e-commerce on your Web site. You may also find it desirable to have a bulletin board on your Web site. Visitors can use the bulletin board to request more information and to share information among those using your products. You can post updates, supplemental assignments, and other resources for students and instructors on your Web site as well. Many publisher Web sites include sample chapters, published reviews, author biographies, and content that visitors can download or a newsletter to which they can subscribe. See, for example, the Web site that my publisher maintains for this book at www.atlanticpathpublishing.com. Creating and managing a successful, content-rich Web site is a complex undertaking, however, and is beyond the scope of this book. The selected resources listed in the chapter appendix are only a start.

Working with Wholesalers and Distributors

Now that you have publicized your book through articles, interviews, presentations, and exhibits; have distributed examination copies; have contacted your potential customers through direct mail and networking; and have developed your Web site as a marketing tool, you now have a basis for reaching out to the publishing community for representation and help.

If a book you self-publish will potentially be stocked by chain stores or independent bookstores, including college stores, you should arrange to have it handled by a book wholesaler and possibly a distributor. While chain bookstores, such as Barnes & Noble and Borders, will special order books from a self-publisher, they probably will not consider stocking them unless they can be ordered from a wholesaler or distributor with whom they deal. It is more cost-effective for resellers (bookstores) to order their stock from one source rather than from thousands of small publishers. Wholesalers and distributors may purchase books directly or on consignment from publishers at a fifty percent or higher discount and usually pay for the books 90 to 120 days after they are sold.

Understanding the Difference

While bookstores order books from both distributors and wholesalers, these entities function differently. Distributors work for publishers. They stock books, handle all aspects of order fulfillment, and actively promote their books to chain and independent bookstores through seasonal catalogs and sales representatives. They usually insist on having the exclusive right to distribute a book and offer assistance in designing an effective cover and planning an effective marketing campaign for it. Examples of distributors of textbooks and academic materials to the library market are Quality Books and Unique Books.

Wholesalers, on the other hand, work for bookstores. They function as order takers. They order books from publishers when bookstores or libraries request them. They do little to promote their books. However, unlike most distributors, they do not require exclusivity. The biggest wholesalers are Baker and Taylor and Ingram. Establishing a business relationship with a wholesaler is an important step in becoming accepted as a small publisher.

In winning trade acceptance, it is important to keep in mind that your book concept actually plays a minor role. The professional appearance of your book, including the cover and interior, the appropriateness of your pricing, and the likely volume of sales are far more important to wholesalers and distributors. There especially must be sufficient perceived demand for a book such as yours in the venues that the wholesaler or distributor serves.

Wholesalers and Distributers: A Comparison		
	Wholesalers	**Distributors**
Whom do they work for?	They work for bookstores and booksellers. They choose what books to accept.	They work for publishers and may specialize in certain markets, such as libraries.
What are their terms?	They do not require an exclusive right to sell your books.	They require the exclusive right to distribute your books, but you can still sell directly.
How do they operate?	They carry a small number of your books on consignment.	They buy and stock your books and sometimes pay for a print run.
How much control do they have over your work?	They do not have or request any rights in your work.	They may request transfer of copyright to them to reprint your book in new editions or other media.
How do they do fulfillment?	They order books from you as needed and sell them at discount.	They fill their customers' orders directly.

Wholesalers and Distributers: A Comparison		
	Wholesalers	**Distributors**
When do they pay you?	They pay you 90 days after they make a sale.	They pay you up front for your books.
How much do they participate in your business?	They usually do not do any marketing or promotion.	They market and promote your book, e.g., through catalog sales.
What do they cost you?	They take a discount of 45% to 60% off your list price.	They take a discount of 60% to 75% off your list price.

Preparing Your Publicity Kit

Wholesalers, distributors, professional reviewers, and interviewers or talk show hosts all will need your publicity kit. Depending on your specific audience, gather the following materials into an attractive presentation folder, as relevant:

- News release, with "For Immediate Release" on the left, contact information on the right
- Headline that relates to news or solves a problem, followed by bulleted points
- Author biography (1-page or full curriculum vitae as needed) and author photo
- Reviews or quotes from reviews
- Suggested interview questions and topical discussion points
- Excerpt from the book
- Press clippings or articles by others for credibility
- Endorsements or testimonials from influential people, media, or customers
- List of clients you have served, workshops you have conducted, or shows you have been on
- Your business card, brochure, flyer, postcard, extra cover or cover photo, or other promotional materials

Include a review copy of your book. Wholesalers and distributors expect to receive these materials. For others, however, query recipients before going to the trouble and expense of mailing out your publicity kit.

Marketing to Academic Libraries

Acquisitions librarians rely almost exclusively on reviews, especially the recommendations of library science specialists and library association publications such as *BookList, Reference and Research Book News,* and *CHOICE.* They attend state, regional, and national library shows where new books are exhibited, and they receive flyers from independent publishers. You should consider participating in these exhibits and mailings.

Libraries also respond to patrons' requests, so you can get your book added to the permanent collection of an academic library by getting people you contact to ask for it, another good use for professional networking. To appeal to the library market, it is important to have CIP or PCIP cataloging information on your copyright page and to include a bibliography and index in your book or academic material.

Marketing to Bookstores

Three types of bookstores through which you may be able to market books are college bookstores, trade bookstores, and Internet bookstores. College bookstores sell both textbooks and professional books. They order textbooks from publishers, used textbook dealers, and wholesalers and distributors after faculty adopt them. College stores especially order through NACSCORP, a company that distributes the products of small and independent publishers and manufacturers to the National Association of College Stores. In addition, all college bookstores are willing to special order upon request any book in print from its publisher. They usually expect a 20 to 30 percent discount on both textbooks and trade books that are special ordered. Trade bookstores, on the other hand, sell mainly books intended for the general public. They do stock some books of interest to a broad range of students and working professionals, such as computer books, but they rarely stock textbooks. Trade bookstores purchase books mainly from distributors and wholesalers.

Using Online Bookstores

Internet bookstores distribute all the books that trade and college bookstores distribute, including textbooks. They are likely to have hundreds of thousands of books available, which online customers find by using powerful search engines. Some books they keep in stock and others they special order. Payment is by credit card. Online catalogs of books include reviews and comments by readers, authors, and publishers.

Incidentally, if you have a Web site for your book but do not want to use it for filling orders, you can link your Web site to Amazon. com's and have them do it for you. Of course, you pay for this service by selling them books at a discount. Consider starting out with Amazon's Advantage program, in which Amazon orders copies on consignment and automatically credits your business checking account monthly with your share of the revenue from sales. I have used Amazon.com to provide information about my books, take orders, do billing and collecting, and arrange for shipping my textbooks. Your online listing should include the following information.

- Author's name, book title, your company's name and address, the date of publication, and the price
- Description of the book's content (including table of contents)
- Photograph of the book's front cover
- Endorsements and quotes from reviews solicited by the publisher
- Unsolicited comments by readers

You provide all the information needed for the listing except, of course, for unsolicited comments. Amazon's Web site provides information on preparing and submitting such listings, for which there is little or no cost.

After books are ordered online, Amazon delivers them. How long it takes to deliver a book depends on the delivery option. The first option is for Amazon to order books from you as they are ordered, in which case you should send copies immediately. The second option is to give Amazon a small number of books (e.g., four) on consignment for them to deliver when they are ordered. When Amazon's stock of your book gets low, they order copies from you to replenish their stock. After your books are paid for (by credit card) and delivered, you receive a check from Amazon, minus its discount, or an electronic deposit of funds directly into your checking account, which is less expensive.

You are not required to give Amazon any exclusive rights to sell your book, and you can have your book sold by other online bookstores as well, such as Barnes & Noble, which very likely will want to order through your wholesalers rather than directly. The following chart compares the cost (at the time of this printing) of having a book listed by Amazon in its two merchant programs. It is worthwhile to list your books on online bookstores. If nothing else, doing so is likely to give your book a little more visibility, thereby yielding some sales that you might not have received otherwise.

Amazon.Com's Merchant Programs		
	Amazon Advantage	*Amazon Marketplace*
Product Lines	Books, Music, & Video	Books, Music, Video, & More
Fulfillment	Amazon.com ships	You ship
Customer Service	Amazon.com provides	You provide
Costs/Fees	$29.94 Annual Fee*	$.99 per sale
Commission Rate	55% or more	15% or more

* Or $39.99 for high volume sellers

Developing Special Promotions

Now you have researched how to reach your customers through libraries and bookstores. Even when you are a vendor partner with a wholesaler and/or online bookstores—or you have a distributor, you still have important marketing tasks. There is more you can do to use the Internet and other mass media to your full marketing advantage.

Email Promotions

Almost all college and university faculty have email addresses. You can use email in at least two ways to market your textbook or instructional material. One is mass emailings to groups that are likely to be interested in your work, being careful to avoid having your email content screened out by spam filters. Email is the electronic equivalent of direct mail marketing. You can also use email to market your textbook or instructional material to individuals in your contact list or in a mailing list that you rent from companies that provide them. It is important to use "opt-in" email addresses, as those individuals have agreed to receive messages like yours.

Another use of email is to post announcements about the publication of your textbook or instructional material on the bulletin boards of relevant newsgroups or listservs, which forward messages to subscribers. It is important to keep announcements brief and to the point and to include ordering or contact information. Some professional and scholarly listservs expressly forbid commercial messages, so you will have to be creative in using this medium to make people aware of the potential usefulness to them of your publications. Asking questions about how list subscribers teach a particular concept or choose instructional materials may be a way to develop contacts for an email promotion.

Radio and Television Promotions

Many authors, including educators and academics, appear on local cable or national network television talk shows and radio shows. Doing so is academically respectable, and media publicity can drive sales of your book. You might research the consortium of college and university radio stations, for instance, to identify possible venues to talk about a subject that relates to your book. With your publicity kit you might interest a public television or public radio host in interviewing you for broadcast. Also see BookTV and Booknet online for more ideas about marketing your book through radio and television promotions.

Book Signings

If you are invited to give a lecture on a subject relevant to your self-published textbook or instructional material, you may want to schedule a book signing following the lecture. Ask the person who invited you to arrange to have someone sell copies at the venue and to publicize before the lecture that there will be a book signing. Advance notice will help ensure that those who want to purchase a copy will have a blank check, credit card, or cash with them. If you have never done a signing and want to see how it is done, attend a signing at your local Borders or Barnes & Noble, or watch Book TV on C-SPAN2, which frequently shows book signings following lectures.

Workshops

The self-published book on which this book is based originally was related to workshops I conducted on academic authoring. I offered three-hour continuing education and faculty development workshops on self-publishing books and materials for students, academics, and professionals, under the auspices of the Text and Academic Authors Association and various colleges and universities that served as host institutions. The workshop was based in part on the book, which was distributed as a handout. The cost of the book was included in the workshop fee. Selling your book or material at your workshop separately is an alternative to using it as a handout. If you sell your book to workshop attendees, consider offering a coupon or discount. Remember to add the names of attendees to your contact list so you can follow up.

Advertising

Ads in professional publications large enough to describe adequately the purpose and content of a textbook or instructional material tend to be expensive. Acquisitions editors for textbook publishers repeatedly have told me that such advertisements rarely yield a sufficient number of orders to recover their cost. However, a small ad in a professional journal that merely announces the publication of your textbook or academic material and refers readers to a Web site where they can get information could yield enough orders to be cost effective.

Advertising in periodicals for college instructors, such as *Academe* or *The Chronicle of Higher Education,* also may be effective. However, advertising works only through repeated exposure, which quickly becomes too expensive, especially for a self-publisher. A 4-inch wide by 4-inch deep black and white ad in *The Chronicle of Higher Education* might cost over $750, and the ad might appear only once! Marketing associations may offer cooperative ads. Also, online advertising on Web sites or keyword-based advertising on search engines such as Google or Overture may prove both affordable and effective. This book has been advertised through Google Adwords.

As you can see, marketing and promotion are key factors in your success as an academic self-publisher. The strategies mentioned in this chapter for marketing textbooks and instructional materials are not the only ones that have been used. Others include donating copies to be auctioned or sold at professional association fundraisers, doing an author tour, entering books in award competitions (e.g., competitions for Texty or McGuffey awards from the Text and Academic Authors Association), having a listing in a mail order catalog for professionals in your field, and distributing books through professional book clubs. As you can appreciate, the work of marketing is never done.

Marketing Resources for Academic Self-Publishers

Selected Sources of Reviews

ForeWord Magazine: http://www.forewordmagazine.com
CHOICE Magazine: http://www.ala.org/Content/
    NavigationMenu/ACRL/Publications/CHOICE/Home.htm
Midwest Book Review: http://www.midwestbookreview.com
SciTech Book News and Reference and Research Book News:
    http://www.booknews.com
H-Net Reviews: http://www.h-net.msu.edu/reviews/
Leonardo Digital Reviews (MIT): http://mitpress2.mit.edu/e-
    journals/Leonardo/ldr.html

Examples of Directories

Books in Print: http://www.booksinprint.com/bip/
Acqweb: http://acqweb.library.vanderbilt.edu/acqweb/pubr.html
Dmoz Open Directory: http://dmoz.org/Business/Publishing_and_
    Printing/Publishers/Directories/
MLA International Bibliography: http://www.mla.org/bibliography
Dustbooks: http://www.dustbooks.com/editdir.htm

Cooperative Marketing Organizations

Small Publishers Association of North America (SPAN): http://
    www.spannet.org
Publishers Marketing Association (PMA): http://pma-online.org

Exhibition Services

Association Book Exhibit (ABE): http://www.bookexhibit.com
Combined Book Exhibit (CBE): http://www.combinedbook.com

Direct Mail Mailing Lists

Quality Education Data (QED): http://www.qeddata.com
Market Data Retrieval (MDR): http://www.schooldata.com
American Library Association: http://www.ala.org/Content/
    NavigationMenu/Our_Association/Offices/Library1/Library_
    Fact_Sheets/mailinglist.pdf

PR and Publicity Leads

PubList: http://www.publist.com

News Directory.com: **http://www.ecola.com**

Center for All Collegiate Information: **http://www.collegiate.net/text.html**

Web US Higher Education Directory: **http://www.utexas.edu/world/univ/**

Higher Education Publications: **http://www.hepinc.com**

Academic Listservs: **http://www.laurentian.ca/library/tools/academiclistserv_e.php, http://www-rohan.sdsu.edu/dept/drwswebb/listservs.html**

LibWeb (Academic Libraries): **http://sunsite.berkeley.edu/Libweb/Academic_main.html**

Television venues for books: **http://www.booktv.org, http://www.booktv.net**

Information on Online Marketing

Bookzone: **http://www.bookzone.com/secret/addresses.html**

Self-Promotion: **http://www.selfpromotion.com**

Barnes & Noble: **http://www.barnesandnoble.com** (Go to "Publisher and Author Guidelines" under "Services")

Amazon: **http://www.amazon.com** (Go to "Advantage" under "Make Money")

Academic Marketing in Canada: **http://www.ualberta.ca/~slis/guides/market/guide.htm**

Selling on Your Web Site: Some Examples

Yahoo e-commerce: **http://smallbusiness.yahoo.com/bzinfo/prod/com**

Web hosting: **http://www.hosting4less.com/ecommerce.html**

E-marketing: **http://www.wilsonweb.com**

Atlantic Path Publishing: **http://www.atlanticpathpublishing.com**

Books and Web Sites on Book Marketing

Marketing Virtual Library: **http://www.knowthis.com**

Marketability: **http://www.marketability.com/publisher.html**

Midwest Book Review Publicity & Marketing: **http://www.midwestbookreview.com/bookbiz/pub_mkt.htm**

Kremer, John, *1001 Ways to Market Your Books,* fifth edition (Open Horizons, 1998).

Reiss, Fern, *The Publishing Game: Bestseller in 30 Days!* (Peanut Butter and Jelly Press, 2003).

Rose, M.J. and Angela Adair-Hoy, *How to Publish and Promote Online* (St. Martin's Griffin, 2001).

Ross, Marilyn, and Tom Ross, *Jump Start Your Book Sales* (Creative Communications, 1999).

Wholesalers

Baker & Taylor: http://www.btol.com/supplier.cfm

Ingram (Section for Small Publishers): http://www.ingrambookgroup.com/Pub_Relations/

Supplier to the National Association of College Stores: http://www.nacscorp.com/ (See "Become a Partner")

Distributors

Quality Books: http://www.quality-books.com

Unique Books: http://www.uniquebooksinc.com/default.asp

Independent Publishers Group: http://www.ipgbook.com/about.html

Sales Representation

National Association of Independent Publishers Representatives: http://www.naipr.org/index.html

12

Financial Considerations for Self-Publishers

inancial aspects of self-publishing include determining the cost of goods sold; pricing books and materials; setting discounts, return policy, and terms for payment; invoicing and shipping; and maintaining adequate financial records for tax and other purposes. Determining the full cost of each book (cost of goods sold) is the first step, and for this you need an inventory of all your business expenses directly tied to publishing your book, such as the cost of marketing it and the cost of manufacturing the book. Divide the total cost by the number of books you have printed. The resulting figure tells you how much you have spent per copy. This figure is the basis for deciding how much to charge for a textbook or instructional material, because you must at least recover this amount to break even. Ideally, you will want a profit margin as well so that you can reinvest in your business. Other factors influencing pricing include how much money you hope to receive for your time and effort, the number of copies you expect to sell, the prices of competing books, what customers expect to pay for a book like yours (i.e., what the market will bear).

Figuring Your Expenses

Consider the following expense categories when figuring the cost of goods sold for purposes of pricing. (For purposes of paying taxes, the cost of goods sold is restricted to costs involved in producing and manufacturing the book as a physical object.)

- Prepublication expenses
- Publication expenses
- Marketing expenses
- Order fulfillment expenses
- Discounts

Prepublication expenses include authoring-related expenses that you would incur even if you were not self-publishing. They include items such as office supplies and equipment, photocopying, travel expenses, graphic artists' fees, permission fees for copyrighted materials, and even your time in drafting your manuscript. Unless you are paying from a grant, you probably will want to charge enough for your textbook or instructional material to at least recover prepublication expenses.

Publication expenses include all expenses incurred with producing and manufacturing a book or material, such as typesetting, copyediting, designing the cover and interior, and the cost of paper, printing, binding, and delivering your order. These expenses also must be recovered.

Add to this your marketing expenses, which can include having brochures or flyers or a catalog designed and printed, renting mailing lists, Web site design and hosting, publicity, exhibiting services, advertising, and so on. The cost of a book manufactured for about $3 per copy might rise to $10 per copy for cost of goods sold when all the expenses are added up.

If you are filling orders yourself and have your inventory on hand, then your order-fulfillment expenses are likely to include invoices, mailing envelopes and boxes, labels, and postage. If, on the other hand, someone else fills your orders, the cost of labor and warehouse space would be additional expenses. Fulfillment houses typically charge a monthly fee, e.g., $40 to $50 a month to store your books, an annual escrow fee for insurance, and additional fees for services performed in filling each order. Order fulfillment includes the cost of postage, shipping, or freight.

You can include shipping charges in the price of a book or material, but this may defeat your pricing strategy. Better to list this separately as a "shipping and handling" fee. Customers expect to pay shipping. If you use direct mail marketing almost exclusively, find an economical way to ship all copies the same way. You could even deliver copies personally if you use them as handouts for a seminar or workshop you conduct.

Note that wholesalers expect you to pay freight charges for books shipped to them on consignment, and these costs must be figured as part of the cost of goods sold. It will be worth your while to find economical solutions for getting your books to your customers.

Another cost of goods sold is the discounts you will have to give to retail resellers—bookstores, which typically get 20 to 40 percent off the cover price. Libraries ordering single copies directly from you expect to pay full price. Most libraries and bookstores order through wholesalers and distributors, however, at deeper discount. As mentioned previously, you will have to give wholesalers 50 percent or more off and distributors even more. As you can imagine, the more direct sales you can make by contacting your potential customers yourself the better.

Figuring Costs: A Typical Ratio	
Prepublication	4,000
Publication	4,000
Marketing	8,000
Fulfillment	4,000
Other	2,000
TOTAL INVESTMENT $22,000	

Figuring Your Price

The amount of money you hope to receive for your time and expertise can range from none to substantial. Writing and self-publishing a textbook or instructional material usually requires a considerable time investment. Whether you hope to profit financially by self-publishing depends, in part, on whether you view the time invested as similar to that for a grant application or a journal article, in which case you may not expect to receive a direct financial reward from it. You may hope to receive indirect financial benefits, however, such as merit salary increases and invitations to give workshops and other presentations for which you receive an honorarium. On the other hand, if you view your time investment in the same way you would a book project for a commercial textbook publisher, you probably would expect to benefit directly from it financially. Regardless, you will almost certainly want to earn enough from sales to cover your expenses, unless you have a grant that will do so.

Your cost of goods sold analysis will tell you your break-even point—the number of copies you must sell in a certain time at a certain price to cover your costs. Beyond that, the more copies you can expect to sell, the lower the price you can charge for each and still make a profit. You would be wise to be conservative when estimating the number of copies you are likely to sell, but not so conservative that the price will be too high and thus discourage sales. Your price also should reflect your competition. That is, your textbook or instructional material should not be priced much higher or much lower than directly competing products.

Psychological variables also influence pricing. Market research indicates that the price charged for a product can affect a consumer's perception of its affordability and quality. For example, consumers tend to judge a product costing $19.95 as significantly more affordable than one costing $20.00. Consumers also tend to question the quality of products that cost considerably less than expected. Finding out what your customers expect to pay for a book like yours is an important part of your market research.

In addition, the industry has certain pricing standards. Adult trade nonfiction books carried by chain stores such as Barnes & Noble are expected to have a cover price of under $20.

Another pricing variable is the likely cost to students of your textbook or instructional material. College stores buy from wholesalers, distributors, and used book dealers at discount and then may mark up the price to students over the cover price.

Some Resources for Financial Management

Definition of Cost of Goods Sold for Tax Purposes: **http://www. ors.gov/**
Free PlanWare for Figuring Working Capital: **http://www. planware.org/workcap.htm**
PMA's articles on a Publisher's Cash Management Plan: **http:// www.pma-online.org/scripts/backissu.cfm**
ABOUT: Marketing: Pricing Strategies: **http://marketing.about. com/cs/advertising/a/pricingstrtgy_2.htm?terms=book+pricing**
Article on the Pricing of University Press Books: **http://aaupnet. org/resources/mellon/bookpricing.pdf**

Setting Your Terms and Conditions

Terms and conditions include, in addition to your discount schedule, your return policy, terms for payment, and billing procedures. Both college and trade bookstores will expect to be able to return for a refund any books that they do not sell. While they are supposed to return books in good condition so that they can be resold, returns sometimes are packed so poorly that they no longer are in salable condition. To give yourself legal grounds for refusing to give refunds on damaged books, you should include a book return policy statement with orders you send to bookstores, distributors, and wholesalers. A sample return policy, along with other terms and conditions, appears in the chapter appendix.

You may also want to have a return policy on books sold to individuals. You can offer a refund if a book does not meet a buyer's expectations. The following notice (based on a similar one in Poynter 1996), for example, appears on the inside front cover of my self-published books:

> CODI Publications is confident that you will find this book to be worth more than your purchase price. If for any reason you do not agree, return the book and we will refund your full purchase price, no questions asked, no reasons requested. The reason we make this unusual offer is that we firmly believe that for any small business to be successful over the long term, it not only needs a quality product but also must go out of its way to provide excellent customer service. This is done by assuring customers in advance that, if dissatisfied with the product, they have easy-to-understand rights to effective recourse. One of these rights is to be able to ask for and receive a full refund.
>
> So, while we look forward to not hearing from you about this guarantee, we will promptly and cheerfully refund your money.

For single-copy sales to individuals, you should insist on prepayment by credit card, check, or money order. Libraries and bookstores sometimes send prepayment with a purchase order number, but often you must invoice them and reference the purchase order number. Wholesalers and distributors usually will not prepay, however. For multiple-copy sales to them and to businesses and institutions, you probably will receive a purchase order and will have to submit an invoice. Try to negotiate for payment within 30 days, but be aware that this is rare in the publishing industry. Wholesalers will take 90 days or longer to pay, and this time is based on the dates they sell the books, not the dates you ship the books to them. Online bookstores such as Amazon.com may not pay initially until your balance due is over $100 after their percentage is deducted, and then, as noted previously, they prefer to pay directly into your business account through electronic transfer.

Filling purchase orders is a routine business operation, and companies and institutions typically honor their obligations to pay for their orders. Many college bookstores will be willing to prepay, however, if asked to do so. Benefits from prepayment include the following.

- Being certain of being paid for books that are ordered and delivered
- Not having to spend time on billing after books are delivered
- Not having to accept returns
- Being able to pay for printing after books have been paid for, if you are printing on demand

For bookstores reluctant to prepay, you may want to offer a benefit for doing so (e.g., not having to pay for shipping). Or, you may be willing to risk and accept a purchase order. Most of them, but not all, are likely to be paid eventually.

Otherwise, billing procedures involve submitting invoices for books and materials for which you received a purchase or a prepayment. You should be able to print suitable consecutive invoices and packing slips with the software you use for maintaining financial records, such as QuickBooks. You also would use this software to record payments and track accounts receivable.

Maintaining Financial Records

You will have to maintain adequate business records for tax and other purposes. If you do not incorporate, you probably will report your income from self-publishing on Schedule C of the federal income tax return. For maintaining your financial records, use a small business software package that does not require an accounting background.

To simplify documenting income and expenses for tax purposes, deposit all of the income you receive from self-publishing to a separate business checking account. For endorsing checks, you might have a self-inking stamp made with PAY TO THE ORDER OF (your bank) or FOR DEPOSIT ONLY (your company account). Pay from this account all the deductible self-publishing-related expenses that you will be claiming on your tax return. If you plan to use a credit card for business purchases, you may want to have one exclusively for this purpose, such as an American Express or other small business card.

No chapter on financial considerations is complete without a discussion of cash flow. Publishing is a type of business in which a great deal of money goes out without hope of immediate or even short-term return. Achieving sales of any volume takes a long time and adds significantly to cost. You probably would not recover you expenses within a year. Thus, if you lack sufficient working capital you will not be able to maintain business long enough to see results. This is true for any business, but more so for book publishers, where the only solution is to keep publishing new titles as an investment in future sales. If you are self-publishing a single textbook or instructional material for limited distribution, however, this cash flow dilemma may not prove to be such a challenge.

Example of a Discount Schedule and Terms

At this time Atlantic Path Publishing offers a 20-25% discount to retail resellers who order direct from the publisher on net 60-day terms. We offer retailers an additional 10% discount on orders of 12 or more books and if we receive payment within 30 days of receipt of invoice.

Single-copy direct sales otherwise are at our full suggested retail price, and the customer pays for shipping. Direct sales of single copies to libraries also are at full retail price. Individual customer satisfaction is guaranteed or your money back.

We also are presently listed with Baker & Taylor and Yankee Peddler Books. Our wholesalers receive 50-55% discounts, free shipping, and net 60- to 90-day terms. Our books are also carried through Barnes & Noble, bn.com, Amazon.com, and other online bookstores. We do not have a distributor at this time.

We presently have a Web site promotion in which we offer a 50% discount to individuals for prepaid prepublication sales of *Self-Publishing Textbooks and Instructional Materials* by Franklin Silverman (one copy per customer via direct sale). That offer expires after February 15, 2004.

In another Web site promotion, until January 31, 2004, we are offering a 20% courtesy discount for direct sales of any of our titles to colleges and universities, academic departments, professional associations, and college textbook publishers ordering 2 or more copies.

Shipping is by USPS by flat rate priority mail or parcel post unless otherwise specified. Shipping by UPS and Fedex also are possible. Any problems with shipping or receiving must be reported to us within 30 days of the order date.

Atlantic Path Publishing is a member of the Publishers Marketing Association and Small Publishers Association of North America. We are interested in participating in catalog sales and in cooperative marketing initiatives and can supply copy and digital photographs. Please contact us.

We can extend credit to retail resellers on recommended accounts involving sales of 2 or more copies, but otherwise retail reseller orders over $50 must be prepaid. This requirement does not extend to wholesalers. Please submit orders on your purchase order form or letterhead.

We accept prompt returns of books (after 90 days but before 180 days of our invoice date) in resalable condition at our expense. Please document returns, listing the quantity and the original invoice number and date. Your account will be credited toward future sales at 100% of the invoice. We do not automatically accept returns of damaged books, as we use packaging that ensures that our books get to you unharmed.

Send returns to M. E. Lepionka, 17 Hammond St., Gloucester, MA 01930.
Orders may be sent to P.O. Box 1556, Gloucester, MA 01931-1556, or use our toll-free phone (877-283-2276) or toll-free fax (866-640-1412). We look forward to doing business with you.

13
Selling Subsidiary Rights for Textbooks and Instructional Materials

W hen you sell a subsidiary right to a textbook or instructional material that you self-published, you enable an entity other than yourself to reprint (reproduce) some or all of it in a particular medium. The entity may be a person or a business. And the right may or may not be limited (e.g., to a specified time period). Subsidiary rights sales that you may be able to make for a textbook or instructional material include the following kinds.

- Reprint rights
- Foreign and translations rights
- Book club rights
- Audio and video rights
- Media and electronic rights
- Licensing
- Serial rights

Reprint Rights

In this type of subsidiary right sale you are granting a publisher exclusive or nonexclusive permission to reprint your book or material in whole or in part. Two types of reprint right are termed hardcover rights and paperback rights, respectively, when a book is being reprinted in a different print format than the original. For anthologies and course packs you may be granting reprint rights for only a chapter or two. One consideration when deciding whether to sell reprint rights is how much the new product could affect your sales. If, for example, permission is requested to reprint the chapters that motivate persons to buy your book, you might refuse unless you were offered a substantial fee. On the other hand, the new product might stimulate sales of your original book rather than detract from sales. Having a chapter reprinted in an anthology or reader could both enhance your professional reputation and sell a few copies of your book that might not have been sold otherwise.

A course pack is a customized anthology used as a textbook at a particular college or university. It consists mainly of reprints of journal articles and book chapters. Pages may be delivered to students bound (like a book) or shrink-wrapped. You may be able to sell nonexclusive rights to parts of your books or materials for course pack adoption. To do so, contact instructors of courses for which your work would be appropriate and inform them about availability for this purpose. Some authors adapt their work for this purpose so that the material can stand alone—i.e., not refer to information presented elsewhere in the book or material.

Foreign and Translation Rights

Two types of foreign rights sales are reprint rights and translation rights. Buying a reprint right enables the purchaser to reprint a book or material as is and sell it in specified countries outside of the United States. Buying translation rights enables the purchaser to translate a book or material into another specified language and to publish and sell copies in that language worldwide.

Authors usually receive both an advance and a royalty on foreign rights sales. The advance is an interest-free loan against royalties that, unlike a grant, may have to be repaid if an insufficient number of copies are sold to pay for the printing. The amount of the advance rarely exceeds the publisher's estimate of first-year royalties less the cost of manufacture. Both advances and royalties usually are negotiable as are other aspects of the publishing contract. Foreign rights sales almost always involve a 50-50 split between author and publisher.

If your interest purely is in disseminating your work, you can encourage translations by sending copies of your English edition to academics and professionals in other countries who might be interested in translating it. This translator then would arrange for publication with a foreign publisher. Your reward would be the satisfaction of seeing your work published in other languages and distributed in other countries with no effort on your part.

You can sell reprint or translation rights directly to foreign publishers. Several trade shows and online rights Web sites focus specifically on the buying and selling of subsidiary book rights. When purchasing translation rights, it is the responsibility of the foreign publisher to find a translator. Textbooks most often chosen for translation are in the sciences or at least do not require insider knowledge of American history, geography, and culture.

Book Club Rights

Most fields have professional book clubs. Many are run by publishers, such as McGraw-Hill or Newbridge. The sale of a book to a professional book club constitutes an independent endorsement of its value and tends to enhance the professional reputation of its author(s). Book club sales may or may not compete with regular sales channels. Ideally, they tend to add on sales that you might not have gotten otherwise. Royalties tend to be low, however, and it is not impossible to saturate one or more of your markets.

To maximize your likelihood of success, at least six months before your publication date, contact book clubs for which your book might stand a reasonable chance of being selected as a main or alternate selection. The sooner the better. Start by sending them information about the book and about you. If they indicate that they are interested in considering the book, you then send them the manuscript or page proofs and possibly also the cover concept.

Book club deals can be of three types. The first is that they print and bind their own copies and pay you a royalty based on their list prices. Book clubs usually also offer an advance. Their royalty rate tends to be lower when a book is used as a premium to subscribers (e.g., as an almost free inducement to join). The second option for such sales is that the book club joins your print run and pays a royalty as noted above. If a book club joins your print run, you will save on production costs because your first printing will be larger. The third option is that the club buys books from you at a set price that includes printing costs and royalty. It may be possible to sell a book to them in this way after it is published.

Media and Electronic Rights

It may be possible to sell reprint rights to text or illustrations from a book or material to an audiobook publisher or to a publisher of instructional audio/video materials. Film rights and performance rights may be more suited to fiction and trade books than to textbooks and instructional materials, but not always.

It may also be possible to sell electronic rights. Digital rights are becoming increasingly viable as a source of income for authors and publishers of textbooks and instructional materials. For example, ebook editions of college textbooks are distributed by charging students to download them to a relatively small and inexpensive microprocessor-based reading device. At least a few publishers have begun distributing college textbooks in both ebook and print editions, and the number doing so is likely to increase. Ebook editions are seen as a way to cope with the loss of income from the sale of used textbooks and as a less expensive way to deliver instruction to learners. Many textbooks are converted to online courses for the same reasons.

Electronic rights also cover the databasing of your content as well as CD-ROM editions, which often can be manufactured and distributed less expensively than print editions. The cost of postage for mailing a book, for example, is greater than that for mailing a disk. Like Web-based applications, CDs offer the capabilities of video, audio, animation, and hyperlinks.

Licensing

Organizations or institutions might seek to license your book or material for their use. The license they purchase enables them to print a certain number of copies and distribute them to a particular group of people. A college that licensed reprint rights for a textbook, for example, would receive a disk containing the files for the book and permission to print up to a certain number of copies for use by students at that institution. The license would forbid selling copies to persons other than students at that institution and it might expire on a particular date. The license could also allow the rights buyer to modify the book in certain ways to tailor it to their needs. For example, chapters might be printed in a different order (and chapter numbers and references to chapters changed) to make the textbook conform to the course syllabus.

Serial Rights

Serial rights are sold to periodicals (e.g., magazines) enabling them to print a chapter or two from a book before the book is published. Some scholarly and instructional books contain material that would be of interest to a segment of the general public and consequently could generate sales of serial rights. Biographies and historical accounts of events are examples. Serial rights normally produce little income, but can sell books by publicizing them. Second serial rights refer to selling rights to periodical publishers after a book has been published. You will need more practical information to be successful at making such sales, however (Kremer 1998). You may find the following chart useful.

Online Resources for Selling Subsidiary Rights

Definitions and examples of subsidiary rights: http://www.henryholt.com/rights.htm

Article for authors on negotiating subsidiary rights: http://www.writersweekly.com/this_weeks_article/000650_09032003.html

Online center for buying and selling rights: http://www.rightscenter.com

PMA's Foreign Rights Virtual Book Fair: http://pma-online.org/pmafair/index.cfm

PubLaw on electronic rights: http://www.publaw.com/erights2.html

PubLaw on licensing: http://www.publaw.com/subsidiary.html

Writer's Toolbag article on negotiating rights fees: http://www.publaw.com/subsidiary.html

Sample Translation Rights Agreement: http://rights.oreilly.com/contract.html

Directory of Book Clubs: http://www.bookclubdeals.com

Articles for writers and publishers on rights and contracts: http://www.ivanhoffman.com/helpful.html

---

14
Selling Your Self-Published Textbook to a Publisher

ome self-publishers, intentionally or not, become publishers when they publish a book that they did not author. I know of several self-publishers, including Prentice Hall, who made this transition successfully. Likewise, the publisher of this book started as a self-publisher. As soon as you agree to publish another author's book, your situation becomes more complex both financially and legally. For example, you now have to negotiate a publishing contract and spend considerable time marketing a book written by somebody else if you want to stand a chance of at least breaking even. I would recommend that you consult an attorney and an accountant before doing so.

For many academic authors, however, self-publishing is a means to an end rather than an end in itself. That is, the reason they self-publish a textbook or instructional material is to establish that there is a sufficient large market to publish it profitably. They hope to sell reprint rights to a textbook publisher rather than continuing to self-publish it or to become a publisher. In addition, some persons who self-publish textbooks or instructional materials eventually find it too difficult, time-consuming, or costly, or they lose interest in marketing the product. These self-publishers would like to sell reprint rights to another publisher.

Selling reprint rights for self-published textbooks or instructional materials to another publisher is entirely possible. First editions of two of the most successful classic textbooks in my field originally were self-published, one in the late 1930s and the other in the 1950s. Revised editions of both books are still in print and have been published for many years by Allyn and Bacon (Pearson Education). Reprint rights to a book I self-published, *Authoring Books and Materials for Students, Academics, and Professionals*, were sold to Praeger.

If you decide to sell reprint rights to your self-published textbook or instructional material, you will need to

- identify possible publishers,
- write query letters,
- prepare a proposal,
- select a submission strategy for the proposal offer, and
- negotiate a publishing contract.

Some guidelines for performing these tasks are summarized here.

Selling Your Book to a Publisher

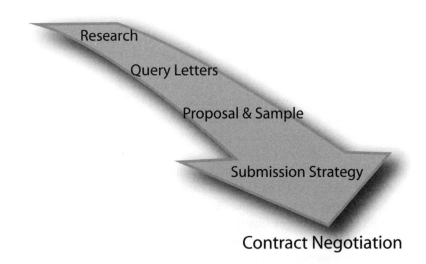

Research

Query Letters

Proposal & Sample

Submission Strategy

Contract Negotiation

Identifying Possible Publishers

There are several types of book publishers, and they can differ from each other in significant ways. Your choice of publisher to approach with a proposal can affect your chances of being offered a lucrative publishing contract.

Publishers of textbooks and professional books are your best bets for successfully selling reprint rights. Textbook publishers publish college or elementary-high school (called el-hi, P-12, or K-12) textbooks. Their marketing focuses on selling books in quantity for course adoptions or to school systems rather than on selling individual copies. Publishers of professional books, on the other hand, focus on marketing books for individual consumers and book clubs. While they certainly are happy to have the books they publish used as course texts, getting such adoptions usually is not their primary marketing focus. For example, publishers of professional books rarely contact professors or distribute examination copies to them.

If your textbook has had a market for both class adoptions and individual sales, you will want a publisher who will market aggressively through both sales channels. In addition, it is essential that the publishers you approach actively market to the niche to which your textbook is likely to appeal. Ideally, publishers have been marketing to this niche for a number of years, and their textbooks or instructional materials are regarded as respectable.

Writing Query Letters

The next step is to send a query letter before sending a proposal package. The reason for sending a query letter first is to determine if a publisher has any interest in acquiring reprint rights to a book such as yours. It would be a waste of time and money to send a proposal package to a publisher who has no interest in giving it serious consideration.

In your query letter, you may want to indicate that the textbook or instructional material has been written and self-published. It would be advantageous to do so if the textbook or instructional material has sold well and if your reasons for wanting to cease self-publishing are credible and academically respectable.

There are several reasons for not bringing out in a query letter that the work is already written and has been self-published. One reason is lack of evidence that the self-published edition sold well. A publisher may hesitate to buy reprint rights to a book or material without convincing evidence (e.g., sales data) that a market exists. Another reason is that acquisitions editors often assume that publishers have necessarily rejected a self-published work. It is unusual in academic and professional circles to undertake such a major project without first receiving a publishing contract. Consequently, an acquisitions editor may assume that another publisher judged the self-publishing book or material as "unsatisfactory" and terminated the contract for it. This mindset reduces the likelihood that your project will be given serious consideration.

For a query letter to be maximally effective, it must:

- Contain a catchy lead that hooks the editor's attention and persuades the editor that the project is both worthwhile and appropriate for his or her list;
- Present compelling evidence that the market for the book or material is sufficiently large to be profitable to publish for;
- Indicate how the book or material compares to competing ones, if any; and
- Establish your authority and credibility as the author.

An effective query letter usually is no longer than one page and is addressed by name to the appropriate editor at the publishing house. Be sure to include copies of reviews, assuming that you have some good ones and are informing the editor that the book was self-published.

Preparing a Proposal

A proposal is a marketing tool. Its main function is to sell publishing rights to a book or material. If it does what it is intended to do, a good proposal will result in an offer of a publishing contract. Perhaps the most important paragraphs in a proposal are intended to convince editors and reviewers that there is a sufficiently large market for the book or material to making its publication profitable. If you fail to convince them of this, you are unlikely to be offered a contract regardless of how good or important the project is or how qualified you are to do it. Consequently, in a proposal for a textbook you should include information about courses for which it could be a required text and the number of institutions that offer such courses.

Your next task is to convince the editors and reviewers who will be evaluating the proposal that you can write well enough and are sufficiently knowledgeable about the topic to deliver an acceptable (satisfactory) manuscript. Your writing ability will be judged by your proposal and sample chapter(s). Acquisitions editors typically send out these materials for peer review to guide their decisions about whether or not to offer you a contract.

After you have established that there is a market for the book and that you have the competence to write it, your next task is to describe or summarize its content and organization, unless you are submitting a copy of your self-published book with the proposal. This information is communicated through a chapter outline and a sample chapter, or chapters. The chapter outline, in addition to its obvious functions, can communicate that you have thought the project through, that there is a book-length work in the idea, and that you have devised the best structure to organize it. The sample chapter (or chapters) provides information about the depth at which material is presented, your points of view, your ability to hold a reader's interest, and the clarity of your writing.

Deciding on a Proposal Submission Strategy

You can submit the proposal to a number of publishers simultaneously or to one publisher at a time. The main advantage of multiple simultaneous submissions is that you are likely to find a publisher sooner, if there is nothing seriously wrong with your proposal. However, if there is something seriously wrong with the proposal, you are more likely to find a publisher using the sequential strategy, because you can use the acquisitions editor's and reviewers' comments to improve the proposal successively, thereby bettering the odds of interesting the next publisher to whom you submit it. Although it may take a little longer to find a publisher using this strategy, your likelihood of eventually finding one is greater than if you use the simultaneous multiple submissions strategy.

Negotiating a Publishing Contract

All publishing contracts are negotiable to some degree. As Michael Lennie, an attorney who specializes in negotiating author-publisher agreements, has stated:

> An offer [of a contract] is an invitation to dicker. A

contract is an agreement. An agreement takes two persons. Publishers do not expect you to sign their standard contract as is. Everything in the contract is negotiable. It is merely their wish list.

The degree to which a publishing contract is negotiable is in part a function of how badly a publisher wants to publish a project and how badly an author wants a publisher to publish it. For example, publishers usually are willing to negotiate more clauses in contracts for textbooks for large enrollment undergraduate courses than for scholarly books unlikely to be big money makers. Nevertheless, publishers are almost always willing to negotiate at least a few of the clauses in contracts for books that they consider likely modest sellers rather than "cash cows."

If you decide to negotiate some of the clauses in a publishing contract, you will have to prioritize the modifications that you want. That is, you will have to decide which of them are so important to you that you would be willing to walk away from the table—not sign the contract—if they are not made. You may find the following resources helpful in negotiating contracts whether you are selling rights as a self-published author or becoming a publisher.

Online Resources for Negotiating Book Contracts

Society of Academic Authors section on Contracts (including clauses, alerts, agents, attorneys, and case law): **http://www. sa2.info/CONTRACTS/**
Article on Book Contract Terms and Royalties: **http://www. fonerbooks.com/contract.htm**
Electronic Issues in Publishing Contracts: **http://www. ivanhoffman.com/electronic.html**
Publishing Contracts and POD: **http://www.adlerbooks.com/ contract.html**
National Writers Union Contracts Glossary: **http://www.nwu. org/bite/gloss.htm**
Publishing Law Center: **http://www.publaw.com**

15
Self-Publishing Trade Books for the General Public

Our focus in previous chapters has been on self-publishing textbooks. Some academic authors have played with the idea of writing trade books, particularly nonfiction ones for children or adults on topics touching on their field of expertise. For example, an entomologist might enjoy publishing a child's book of bugs, or a psychologist might want to publish a trade book of practical tips for conducting relationships. Like textbooks, such trade books can be self-published. One reason that an academic may choose to self-publish a trade book is that they may find it quite difficult to get a publishing contract in a genre when they already have a strong national reputation as a textbook author. Much of the information in this book also is applicable to self-publishing nonfiction trade books.

The main differences in marketing between trade books and textbooks include the following among others.

- Size and cover design
- Print runs and pricing
- Publicizing
- Direct sales
- Selling to book stores and other retail outlets
- Selling to public libraries
- Selling reprint rights

This chapter summarizes these differences.

Size and Cover Design

It is important that any trade book you self-publish be similar in appearance to those of the same genre that are published commercially by other publishers. Your trade book should be the same trim size and have a cover that is similar to others in both design and content. The four most common trim sizes used for trade books are 4- x 7-inches, 5.5 x 8.5, 6 x 9, and 8.5 x 11. The 4 x 7 trim size is used primarily for inexpensive, mass-market paperbacks. Most other trade books are either 5.5 x 8.5 or 6 x 9. Of the two, the 5.5 x 8.5 is the most economical to print and bind.

Cover design and layout are just as important in marketing trade books as in marketing textbooks. While it is certainly true that "you can't judge a book by its cover," marketing research nevertheless indicates that a trade book's cover definitely has an impact on its sales, particularly if it is sold primarily through bookstores and other retail outlets. If the front cover is attention grabbing, and if it is shelved face out, it will be picked off the shelf and glanced at more often than otherwise. In addition, the title on the spine must be large enough to be read from a distance of 6 feet.

The content and layout of a trade book's back cover also is important. The information it presents about a book's content and author should motivate a relatively high percentage of people who read the back cover to purchase the book. One way to determine if your cover and back cover copy are likely to enhance sales is to get reactions from a focus group before you commit to print. In addition, it is crucial that a book's ISBN number and barcode appear at the bottom of the back cover. Trade bookstores and other retail outlets will not stock books without barcodes.

Print Runs and Pricing

Trade books typically are produced in greater quantities to keep unit cost low. A print run of 10,000 to 100,000 copies would not be unusual, for example. Even so, because the discounts demanded by the distributors and wholesalers can exceed fifty percent, many trade book publishers price their books at three or five times the manufacturing cost. They believe that doing so enables them to offer books to retailers at high discounts, to publicize and market the titles adequately, and still make a reasonable profit. While textbook publishing is driven by course adoptions, trade book publishing is driven almost exclusively by volume sales to individuals.

Publicity

"Publicity is doing good and then telling the world about it" (Kremer, 1998, p.159). You create demand for a self-published trade book by letting people know about it, particularly those who are highly likely to have an interest in the subject. Trade bookstores may be willing to stock a self-published book (especially if it does not appear to be self-published) if there appears to be a demand for it. Consequently, if you want to maximize the likelihood of having a book stocked by trade bookstores, you must assume the responsibility for aggressive publicity and promotion.

Approaches used to publicize a trade book include the following.

- Have the book reviewed in newspapers, magazines, newsletters, and on Web sites that people who are interested in the subject matter are likely to read.
- Get news and feature write-ups about yourself, your company, and your book in newspapers and on Web sites in which the book is mentioned.
- Send a professional publicity kit and sample copy to book buyers and other decision makers.
- Do interviews on radio talk shows about the subject of the book, possibly via telephone, and investigate ways to get some television exposure as well.
- Offer lectures or seminars to groups about the book, possibly followed by a book signing.
- Conduct an author tour.

In addition, a professional publicist or literary agent can help a self-published author.

Direct Sales and Sales to Retailers

Some trade book authors (including professors) have sold thousands of copies of their self-published trade books by loading copies into the trunk of their car and calling on persons who would be likely to purchase them. Likely customers include people associated with municipal libraries, such as acquisitions librarians. They also include persons attending meetings of organizations or associations that have the subject matter as a focus. Furthermore, you may attempt to place copies of your books (at a discount or on consignment) with independent trade bookstores or other retail outlets. Also, as with textbooks, trade books can enjoy direct sales through e-commerce Web sites.

To have your book stocked (not merely special ordered) by trade bookstores, you will have to offer it at a fairly large discount. In addition, you will have to document that the book has been and will continue to be publicized sufficiently to create a demand. However, many retail stores that are not bookstores sell books. Mass market and trade books are sold in drug stores, department stores, and gift shops, for example, and children's books are sold in children's clothing and furniture stores as well as toy stores. Likewise, cookbooks often are sold in kitchen goods stores. If a trade book you self-publish is likely to interest patrons of a particular type of store, you may be more successful marketing books in this way than through bookstores. There are at least two reasons. First, it is unlikely you will have to offer as large a discount. And second, it is more likely that you book will be displayed prominently.

Sales to Public Libraries

There are approximately 9,000 public library systems in the United States (See **http://www.publiclibraries.com**). And all of them purchase trade books for their general collections. Most of the books and periodicals that public libraries purchase are ordered from library wholesalers or distributors rather than directly from publishers. Doing so simplifies and centralizes the ordering process for them. Consequently, to be successful selling significant numbers of your books to public libraries, you will have to arrange to distribute to them through the wholesalers with whom they deal. Furthermore, you will have to make them aware of your book. One of the best ways to do this is to have it reviewed in one or more of the review journals that librarians from public libraries consult routinely when deciding which books to acquire. See, for example, the various publications of the American Library Association (ALA, **http://www.ala.org/**). It is also important to exhibit your trade book in national and regional library shows.

Sales of Reprint Rights

Self-publishing a trade book can be an end in itself or a means to interest a publisher in it. It is easier to sell reprint rights for a trade book if you can document that it can be profitable. Trade book publishers will be interested if you can report strong sales of your self-published edition. Publishing decisions for trade books usually are made without input from outside evaluators. This differs from the usual practice of peer review in academic, professional, and textbook publishing. Trade book editors rely on literary agents to screen out projects that are not of sufficiently high quality or are inappropriate for their firm. Consequently, you may want to try to interest a literary agent in your project, especially if you can document that your self-published edition sold well.

Your trade book might be a spin off of your textbook project. Professional memoirs, popularizations of academic subjects, and perspectives on popular culture have gained greater acceptance in scholarly circles during the last decade. And demand for these books among the public has increased, as a glance at the nonfiction bestseller lists will show (e.g., see *Publishers Weekly*, **http://www.publishersweekly. com**, and the *New York Times Book Review*, **http://www.nytimes.com/ pages/books/**).

References and Bibliography

Applebaum, J. (1988). *How to Get Happily Published*. New York, NY: Harper & Row.

Beach, M. and E. Kenly (1999). *Getting It Printed: How to Work with Printers and Graphic Imaging* (3rd edition). Cincinnati, OH: North Light Books.

Dible, D. M. (1978). *What Everyone Should Know about Patents, Trademarks, and Copyrights*. Fairfield, CT: Entrepreneur Press.

Famous Writers School (1969). *Principles of Good Writing*. Westport, CN: Famous Writers School.

Kremer, J. (1998). *1001 Ways to Market Your Books* (5th edition). Fairfield, IA: Open Horizons.

Larson, M. (1985). *How to Write a Book Proposal*. Cincinnati, OH: Writer's Digest Books.

Lepionka, M. E. (2003). *Writing and Developing Your College Textbook*. Gloucester, MA: Atlantic Path Publishing.

Luey, Beth (2002). *Handbook for Academic Authors* (4th edition). New York: Cambridge University Press.

Michener, J. A. (1992). *James A. Michener's Writer's Handbook*. New York: Random House.

Miles, J. (1987). *Design for Desktop Publishing: A Guide to Layout and Typography on the Personal Computer*. San Francisco, CA: Chronicle Books.

Miller, C. and K. Swift (1988). *Handbook of Nonsexist Writing: For Writers, Editors, and Speakers* (2nd edition). New York: Harper & Row.

Parsons, P. (1989). *Getting Published: The Acquisition Process at University Presses*. Knoxville, TN: University of Tennessee Press.

Poehner, D. and S. Spears, eds. (2003). *2003 Photographer's Market*. New York: Photographer's Market.

Poynter, D. (1996). *The Self-Publishing Manual* (9th edition). Santa Barbara, CA: Para Publishing.

(2002). *The Self-Publishing Manual* (13th edition). Santa Barbara, CA: Para Publishing.

Poynter, D. and D. O. Snow (2000). *U-Publish.com*. Bloomington, Indiana: Unlimited Publishing.

Radke, L. F. (1996). *The Economical Guide to Self-Publishing*. Chandler, AZ: Five Star Publications.

Reiss, F. (2003). *The Publishing Game: Bestseller in 30 Days!* Newton, MA: Peanut Butter and Jelly Press.

Rose, M .J. and A. Adair-Hoy. (2001). *How to Publish and Promote Online*. New York: St. Martin's Griffin.

Ross, M. and T. Ross (1999). *Jump Start Your Book Sales*. Buena Vista, CO: Creative Communications.

Ross, T. and M. Ross. (1994) *The Complete Guide to Self-Publishing*. Cincinnati, OH: Writer's Digest.

Silverman, F.H. (1998). *Authoring Books and Materials for Students, Academics, and Professionals*. Westport, CT: Praeger.

(1999). *Publishing for Tenure and Beyond*. Westport, CT: Praeger.

Strunk, W., Jr., and E. B. White (2000). *The Elements of Style* (4th edition). Boston: Allyn and Bacon.

Vogele, S. (1992). *Handbook of Direct Mail*. London, England: Prentice Hall International (UK) Ltd.

Williams, R. (1990). *A Mac Is Not a Typewriter*. Berkeley, CA: Peachpit Press.

(1994). *The Non-Designer's Design Book*. Berkeley, CA: Peachpit Press.

(1995). *The PC Is Not a Typewriter*. Berkeley, CA: Peachpit Press.

Index

CD-ROMs, 25; 64; 83-87
Clip art, 101-102
CODI Publications, 13; 155
Comb binding, 77
Communication software, 64
Compression software, 83
Computer Hardware, 50-51;
61-62; 64
Contracts, publishing, 171-
172
Contrast in page design, 98-
99
Convention (conference)
papers, 4-5; 26; 87; 134-135
Copyediting, 33; 53
Copyright, 119-125
    Deposit of, 125
    Duration of, 121
    Forms for, 128
    Guidelines for, 121-
    124
    Infringement of,
    125-126
    Transfer of, 123
Copyright Act of 1976, 119-
126
Copyright notice, 125
Copyright page, 20; 110
Copyrighting a self-published
work, 10; 21; 52; 119-125
Corporation, 43
Cost of goods sold, 151-153
    For pricing, 151-154
    For taxes, 151
Course packs, 162
Covers for books, 20; 31-32;
78-79
Cover design, 31; 34
Cropping (illustrations), 101-
103

D-E

Daily writing schedule, 59-61
DBA (doing business as), 44
Dedication page, 20; 110-111
Deductions, for home business,
41
Digital
    Books, 83-85
    Files, 102-105
    Media, 87-88; 90
Direct-mail marketing, 136-137
Disclaimer, 20; 112
Discount Schedule, 158-159
Discounts, 153; 176
Distribution, 138
Distributors, 138-140; 149; 156
DPI (dots per inch), 34-35; 50;
104-105
Drafting text, 61-64; 65-67
Drawings, 29-30; 68-69
Dust jackets, 31-32; 34
EAN Bookland Barcode, 51-52
Ebooks, 25; 83-86
E-commerce, 56-57
Editing text, 65-67; 71
Editorial style, 67
Electronic publishing, 19-20; 83-
86; 89-90
Electronic rights, 164
E-mail marketing, 143-144
Encryption, 83-84
End notes, 115
End matter, 115
Endorsements, 131-132
Endpapers, 110
Epigraph, 110-111
Examination copies, 135

Ink used for, 75-76
On demand, 10; 80-82; 89
Trim sizes for, 74
Preparing pages for, 19-20;
Paper used for, 75-76
Photo-offset process, 73-74
Production tasks, 21; 32-35
Profitability, 154-154
Professional books, 163; 169
Professional meetings, role of, 4-5; 26; 87; 134-135
Proportional (and non-proportional) fonts, 92-93
Proposals, book, 170-171
Profitability, 38
Proximity in page design, 98-99
Public domain, 122
Public libraries, 176-177
Publicity, 14; 140-141; 147-148
Publishers
Academic and scholarly, 4-5; 28
Textbook, 3-5; 8-10; 11-12; 169
Trade book, 173
Publisher's Cataloging in Publication (PCIP), 52; 126
Publishers Marketing Association (PMA), 135; 147
Publishing
    Alternatives, 19; 38-39
    Company set up, 13; 18-19; 41-54; 55-57
    Contract, 171-172
    Software, 34; 48-49; 50-51; 56-57; 64-65; 71-72; 114
Purchase orders, 155-156

Q-S

Query letters, 169-170
Radio promotions, 144
Ragged right, 96-97
References, 115-116
Registering a self-published work, 21; 55-56; 126; 128
Repetition in page design, 98-99
Reprint rights, 22; 161-162; 177
Resale permit, 43
Respectability of self-publishing, 1-5; 26-27
Retail outlets, 175-176
Retail price, 176
Returns, 155-156
Reviews, 15; 133; 147
Revisions, 10
Rights sales, 177
Royalties, 163
Royalty financing, 47-48
Running foot (and running head), 96
Saddle stapling, 78
Sales tax, 43
Sans serif, 91-92
Satisfactory manuscript, 9
Scanners, 102-103
Schedule C, 28; 156-157
SCORE (Service Corp of Retired Executives), 43-44
Script fonts, 91-92
Second color, 31; 76
Self-publishing; 39; 55-57
    Respectability of, 1-5; 26-27
    Benefits of, 7-12
    Risks of, 13-15

T-Z